Twice Chosen

Twice Chosen

One Woman's Story of Healing

By
Betsy Schenck Kylstra

Twice Chosen
One Woman's Story of Healing

Author: Betsy Schenck Kylstra

Published by: Proclaiming His Word Publications
2849 Laurel Park Highway
Hendersonville, NC 28739
828-696-9075
877-214-8076
office@phw.org
www.phw.org

Former
Address: PO Box 2339
Santa Rosa Beach, FL 32459

Edited by Chester D. Kylstra, Dody Griffith, Jeannie Clark and Marge Wolfe.

Cover Art by David Murray.

Unless otherwise noticed, Scripture quotations are from the King James Version of the Bible.

Third Printing, March 2005

Paperback Edition, -3, September 1996.

ISBN 0-9649398-5-1

Table of Contents

PART I

Twice Chosen

One Woman's Story of Healing

Table of Contents (Continued)

Table of Contents (Continued)

PART 2

Twice Chosen

God Proves His Faithfulness

Table of Contents (Continued)

PART 3

Twice Chosen

Into the Future

Foreword

You will be blessed and enlightened as you read this book. It will cause you to laugh and to cry. It will cause you to contemplate and meditate on God's goodness and faithfulness.

Twice Chosen gives a vivid portrayal of God's providential purpose being worked out in an individual's life. Betsy's life reveals that God chooses us before we know we have been chosen. It demonstrates God's timing and seasons that cause things to happen in a chain of events to bring one forth to divine destiny.

I have known Betsy and Chester long enough to assure the reader that Betsy is a living testimony of God's grace, love and faithfulness. Her life reveals many of the divine principles that are used to take a woman from "Called to Be" to "Being Commissioned" to fulfill God's purpose for her existence on earth. Chester's insight into their learning God's truth of sowing and reaping is a key to their success in their life and ministry.

Jesus Christ has given Chester and Betsy a ministry that is near and dear to His heart. God spoke to me in the mid 70's, that the 1990's would be the decade that brought forth His prophetic ministry and His counseling ministry. Chester and Betsy have been divinely directed to bring these two ministries together. It has resulted in one of the most effective ministries ever to be brought forth in Christ's Church.

God bless you, Betsy, for sharing your life with us. Your testimony, and the resulting counseling ministry, will bless hundreds of thousands around the world.

Bishop Bill Hamon
June, 1996

Dedication

I joyfully dedicate this book to Chester, my husband, my friend and the love of my life. This story is my story and yet in a greater sense it is also our story.

Life has been much more richer because of your love, much more challenging because of your belief that I can do the impossible and much more of an adventure because of your steadfast faith in God's call.

Acknowledgments

So many things in my life are the result of the combined effort of many special people who know, love and continue to support me.

Thank you, Lois Blanchard and Steve Bishop, for running the ministry office and tactfully protecting me from the phone, so that I could write. Thank you, Dody Griffith, for your editorial skills and suggestions and for your total willingness to "read the manuscript one more time." Thank you too, for the times I heard you laughing or "sniffling" as you typed in the latest chapter at the computer. Your response encouraged me to keep going. Thank you, Jeannie Clarke, for applying your excellent editing skills.

Thanks go to my trusted friends Patty Overholt, Polly Altman, Steve and Cindy Bishop, Paul and Julie Metcalf, Katie Metcalf, Jackie Varnedoe, Bishop Hamon and my own son Lewis Davis, who read through the first draft of this manuscript and gave me candid comments that greatly enhanced this book.

Thank you, David and Mary Ellen Murray, for taking a concept and translating it into a wonderful design for the book cover.

Thanks most of all to you, Chester, for hours of editing, formatting and encouraging. Thank you for continuing to say to me, "Honey, you are a natural-born story-teller. All you have to do is just write it down instead of speaking it out loud!"

Preface

Even now, it seems strange to be writing a preface to a book. Until two years ago, I never had the least inkling that anyone, other than my immediate friends, might be interested in my life.

The Lord must see it differently. Over the past two years, three prophets have given me prophetic words about writing an autobiographical account of my life.

The last prophet, Steve Schultz, put it so unthreateningly:

> I also feel like the Lord is saying that there is a book in you, Betsy. There is a testimonial book that needs to be written; not a very large one, but something where people can get to know you and the ministry that you and Chester have.

I grabbed on to the phrase "not a very large one," which gave me courage to proceed.

I have enjoyed the writing process. I have made the focus "my much needed healing." As I share with you, dear reader, some of the special things that the Lord has done in my life, my prayer is that you will find fresh hope and be touched again by God's goodness.

Betsy S. Kylstra
September, 1996

Addendum to Preface

It is very satisfying to me that *Twice Chosen* is going into its third printing. Many thanks to all of you who have expressed appreciation for this book and its impact on yours and other's lives.

Much has happened in the eight years since the initial release of this book in 1996. Too much to add here. Let me just state that the Healing House Network is growing, providing healing and freedom to many in the Body of Christ.

Also, the many prophecies concerning a training center are now a reality, creating a whole new set of testimonies of God's goodness and His faithfulness. We moved to Hendersonville, NC, the middle of 2004 and established the Restoring the Foundations International Training Center at Echo Mountain Inn. It is about time for another book to update all that He has done, as He has led us by His voice on a prophetic journey. However, for now, let me direct you to the author's page (page 177) where I have listed our updated contact information including the web sites for the three primary ministries.

Betsy S. Kylstra
March, 2005

PART 1
of

Twice Chosen

One Woman's Story of Healing

By Betsy Schenck Kylstra

My Father's Blessing

It was a bright, sunny day, November 1985, in Pensacola, Florida. I had just returned home from the Bible College where I was both taking classes and teaching. My Wednesday morning class had gone well and I was making plans for next week's class, when the telephone rang.

"You better come as soon as you can," were my mother's words.

I knew exactly what she meant. As I prepared to fly to Charlotte, North Carolina, I packed for a funeral.

My father, age 87, had been sick for six months. Arriving home late that afternoon, I sat quietly as I reached through the bars of his hospital bed to hold his warm, familiar hand. The afternoon sunlight filled his cheerful bedroom and seemed incongruent with the gravity of his condition.

Dad, who had been quiet for a while, opened his eyes and began to reminisce. He started talking about the years he taught Bible at Davidson College and how many of "his boys" had gone into the ministry; about his much-loved grandchildren and about special trips he had taken with us and with my mom.

"You know, she's still as pretty as she always was," he mused, looking tenderly over at her. Mother smiled. She always enjoyed his appreciation. Then Dad's mind locked in on a long forgotten event of my life; an event that happened when I was only twelve. "Do you remember, Betsy, what you said to me the night you went up to the altar at the Billy Graham crusade?"

"No, Daddy, I don't," I replied. I remembered feeling like Jell-O that night, but nothing about our conversation.

"You said, 'Daddy, I know I've already given my life to Jesus, but I wanted to do it one more time, because Daddy, I just don't want to miss anything!'"

1

His face lit up, like the sun emerging from behind a cloud, coming into full brightness. Turning his head to look at me directly, he spoke with a gentle intensity, measuring and emphasizing each word.

"Sugar," he said, "I want you to know that you haven't missed anything!"

His quiet, reflective words wrapped an endorsement around my life; an endorsement of his love and his appreciation. His father's heart had cherished the words of his twelve-year-old daughter for over thirty-three years. My father, who knew my failures as well as he knew my victories, was giving me his final, "Yes and Amen." His final blessing.

Less than a week later, I was sitting on the front row of the Davidson College Presbyterian Church. I was grieving, but, at the same time, also celebrating his life. James and Lewis, my two college-age sons, agreed to sing at their grandfather's funeral. Vibrant with life and emotion, their voices rang out filling the church.

How firm a foundation ye saints of the Lord, is laid for yourselves in His excellent Word ...

This song so simply summed up my dad's life, my precious daddy, who had spent his life teaching and living out of God's Word.

Then came the words I had anticipated. These were words he had shared with me much earlier, words I knew he had chosen to be read on this day.

And so we come today not to chant a dirge, but to sing a song; not to bow in defeat, but to exalt in victory; not to write an end, but to shout a beginning; not to record a death, but a coronation.

"Yes, Dad," I whispered, "thank you for blessing my life so greatly and for such a rich heritage of faith. Daddy, I'll always love you."

Twice Chosen

Actually, my father's blessings had begun many years earlier, in 1940. What a surprise my mother had in late October that year, getting a call from the North Carolina Children's Home Society, an adoption agency.

"We have a little girl for you," they said.

"A little what? A little girl?" my mother questioned, the shock evident in her voice.

My parents had adopted a son, Charlie, three years earlier and had applied for another little boy to keep him company.

"Ah, well, yes. Yes! We will come immediately."

My mother left what she was doing, drove to the college where my father taught and announced to him and his class,

"Lewis, come quickly, we have a little baby girl!"

Daddy made history that day by dismissing class, not even giving his students a homework assignment. Full of emotion, my parents cautiously tried out the words, "We have a little girl."

When they arrived in Greensboro later that day, the busy social worker told them to go into the nursery where the babies who were waiting to be placed were kept. Five or six tiny ones lay in bassinets, awaiting decisions that would affect their destinies. My parents looked carefully at each baby, then stopped and stood by me.

"This is the daughter the Lord has given us," they said to each other.

They knew immediately that I was theirs. With a sense of divine purpose, they chose me. It was settled in their hearts. In a few minutes, the social worker came in to provide confirmation that the baby they were looking at was indeed the one for them. She also added that an unusual thing had happened.

"The birth mother of this baby sent along a lot of sweet baby clothes. Would you like to see them?" she asked.

My parents shared the good news of my adoption with me very early in my life, the news that I was especially chosen.

"If we could have picked from all of the little girls in the world, we would have picked you. God made you just for us and you are perfect for us." Then they added, "You know, other parents have to just take whatever baby they get. They don't have any choice, but **we got to choose you.**"

It made me feel very, very special. It made me feel that I was important. Eventually, it made me feel that God had such a specific plan for my life that He needed to take me out of one family and put me into this one, so that His plan would work out just right. I had a deep, unspoken sense of destiny. I was special, especially picked out, especially chosen.

So I began a rich love relationship with my parents that grew and flourished through the years. This love would help heal many of the wounds and insecurities already present within their tiny baby girl. This love would help lay a foundation of understanding within me so that later I could receive God the Father's love and His Choosing.

As I came to know the Lord, I realized that, just as my parents, **He had also chosen me**. That was good news. In a wonderful way, I already understood early in life what it meant to be chosen. It meant that I was very special, very loved and that I had a unique destiny.

Before I was school age, my parents read to me directly from the Bible.

"Listen to this, Betsy, it says here that the Lord has blessed us with every spiritual blessing:

> Just as He **chose us** in Him before the foundation of the world, He predestined **us to adoption ...** to Himself, according to the kind intention of His will."[1]

I understood. It was good. I loved being twice adopted, **twice chosen.**

---

[1] Ephesians 1:5

Davidson

"Welcome to Davidson. This is your new home."

These were my three-year-old brother's warm and welcoming words to me, all six pounds of me, as I unknowingly arrived in Davidson, December, 1940. I settled into the big house on Woodland street, which was to become my be- loved home. Within its walls, my parents would love and enjoy me, correct and guide me, and lay godly foundations in my life.

My Home

My house itself was a two-story, engaging, white-frame Williamsburg-style house, with dormer windows and deep green blinds and split cypress wooden shingles. It always smelled fresh and alive, for mother made beautiful arrange- ments of colorful garden flowers in the summer and of pine and cedar from our hillside in the winter. The inside of my house was painted Williamsburg blue, or blue and white. There were deep reds in the upholstered furniture, as well as touches of green. Usually there were hints and waifs of cinnamon or something irresistibly enticing coming from the kitchen. This was especially true over weekends and holidays.

Off of our spacious living room and dining room, overlooking the hillside and woods, was our big back porch. Its ceiling was three stories high and it was filled with wonderful lacy-looking wicker furniture; "The good kind," Mother used to say. Here we lounged, spring and summer, enjoying the cool of the green gray flagstone floor on our bare feet. Pots of sweet smelling petunias and scarlet geraniums lined the steps from the house to the porch.

My room was always upstairs on the second floor. Early in my life it had pink rosebud wall paper. My room was almost full with my bed, my little roll top desk and my blue doll bed filled with varieties and vintages of dolls. Later, Daddy painted my room light blue and made matching painted hanging shelves for my teacup collection. Mother and I picked out a blue and lavender flowered bedspread and pillows. I couldn't wait for my friends to see my room. By day, it was my wonderful haven. I delighted in everything about my house, my home.

My Town

I also loved my small, endearing town. Its southern atmosphere was warm and genuinely friendly. It was child safe. The houses were close together and the neighbors that lived on either side of us, up and down the street, were our friends. We borrowed a lemon or a cup of sugar from Mrs. Betty, rather than making a five-minute trip to the store. When anyone was sick, we shared food. We kept each other's house keys in case there was an emergency when someone was away. Actually, however, no one ever locked their homes unless they were going out of town. If I were out playing in the street and it was past six o'clock, one of the neighbors would say,

"Betsy, you're going to be late for dinner. Go home now."

I would obey. Our neighbors were friends, our extended family.

It was safe to ride my bike to see my girl friends, Deedie Withers and Mary Caroline McCutchan, safe to go to the tennis courts and safe to ride downtown. I had lots of downtown friends.

"Let's see, it's box 21, isn't it, Missy?" the Postmaster would say.

"Yes sir," I would reply. Of course, "it" had been box 21 for over fifty years. One summer I got a letter addressed "to Betsy from Evelyn." I felt so important. Just think, I was the main "Betsy" that the Postmaster knew!

The shop keepers were my friends also: Mr. Goodrum at the drugstore; Mr. Mckissick, whose shoe repair shop always smelled of hot machinery, leather and shoe polish; and Mr. Walter Henderson, who repaired my watches free. He would peer out from behind his jeweler's glasses and comment,

"You're looking more and more like Princess Margaret every day."

I wasn't exactly sure who Princess Margaret was, but it was ever so flattering to think I looked like princess "anybody."

One day I went to the bank where my friend Mr. Lore worked. "I want to put all my money somewhere where my parents can't borrow it," I told him confidentially, handing him my hard-saved five dollars. With utmost respect, he received my money. In a few minutes, Ms. Eugenia Deaton smilingly handed me a tan, crisp bank book. It showed that my five dollars were now safely in Mr. Lore's bank.

There were other friends too, at church and at the college where Daddy worked. When I had the measles, Mrs. Cunningham, the college president's wife, brought me over her treasured scrapbook of angels. There were pictures of stiff Byzantine ones, larger-than-life Renaissance ones and even some modern angels, depicted in stain glass windows.

Mother thought that it was an awfully special thing for her to do. So, I wrote Mrs. Cunningham a long thank-you note, trying to sound pleased.

I liked seeing the same people downtown, in my church and at the college. I felt at ease, secure. It was as if my happy Davidson was covered with a canopy of beneficent protection. Its borders represented a soothing safety net within which I was known and loved. Its consistently sheltering arms helped me believe that life was good and that people were caring and trustworthy. Davidson instilled optimism about my future and, in my early years, a deep sense of belonging. Many days I carried within myself that snugly protected feeling described so well in Browning's poem, *Pippa Passes*:

God's in His Heaven, All's right with the world.

Perhaps my life in Davidson was traditional, but it was "traditional good." Until my college years, I did not know even one person who was divorced. I thought "Davidson life" was the way everybody lived!

My First Love

It was in Davidson that I experienced my first love. Sometime during my teens, the rest of my face caught up with my nose and life began to normalize. Gradually, I began leaving behind my unselfconscious tomboyish ways and activities and entered into a new realm: the enchanting realm of boys. I remember the day it happened.

I was swinging in the Eberhardt's hammock with David, Jonathan and D. G. Martin. We were flying frighteningly high in the air, daring each other to jump out.

"Last person out is a rotten egg," Jonathan yelled tauntingly.

"Not me," I screamed back, plummeting myself into the air and landing in a hole a few feet away, dug out by our antics. D. G., next to bail out, joined me as we waited to see who was going to be the rotten egg. Just as Jonathan made the leap, D. G. asked,

"Are you coming to church tonight? If you'd like to come, I'll ask my parents if I can walk you home afterwards."

I looked at him, his face rosy with exertion, his sturdy body already becoming tall and strong. I noticed his clean cut features, the sparkle in his eyes, his large hands. A split second before, he had been no more than my friend, my competitor in a game. Now he was something mysterious, something different from me: "a boy."

"I would like to go," I said. "I'll run home and ask if I can."

Something deep in my stomach stirred. It wasn't exactly a pain. It felt as if some unidentified, amorphous thing that had for years been lying contentedly below the surface, was waking up, taking shape and coming voluntarily to the surface of my life. I started up Schenck's Hill in my usual gallop. Suddenly, I slowed down. I slowed all the way to an almost demure, almost feminine, walk.

An unfamiliar thought came to me. "What shall I wear tonight?" I looked down at my familiar regulars: my tee shirt and boy's blue jeans with the fly in the front. "I think I might wear my new, pale-green sun dress; that is, if Mother lets me go."

She did, and I did. I don't remember who was the rotten egg.

This was the beginning. It was the summer of my seventh-grade year.

It was several more years before D. G. and I began dating. He became more than my friend. We would sit together on the school bus and dance close at parties at Erwin Lodge. I cheered for him until I was hoarse at all of the North High ball games. After summer football practice, he would ride by our house in his family's station wagon and lean on the horn. Heart palpitating, I would rush to the upstairs window, trying to catch a glimpse of him.

Sometimes, we would put my 45 rpm record of *Unchained Melody* on the record player and dance in our kitchen, with my mother appearing every fifteen minutes, "to see if we needed anything." On our weekend dates, we drove around singing tunes from musical shows. He perfected driving with one arm over my shoulder. I enjoyed all the delicious, tingly sensations of excitement. D. G. became my special confidant, my dear friend, my first love.

Perhaps there is nothing that special or unique to describe, yet for me, it was such a formative relationship. The genuineness of our love touched my life deeply. At a time when I was learning about trust in relationships, D. G. was always trustworthy. At a time when I was risking giving my heart, he treated it with tenderness. At a time when I was struggling with issues of value, he treated me with respect and affection. The tone of our relationship harmonized with the tones of Davidson: kind, stable and secure.

Being a class ahead of me, D. G. graduated and went to college first. Although our relationship was already coming to an end, I still felt lost and alone without him. I grieved much of my senior year.

Someone once asked me why we never got back together again. I believe it was because God had different purposes for our lives. But D. G. was part of what made Davidson so good.

Christian Foundations

My parents were godly people. My dad, Lewis Schenck, had gone to seminary and at one time thought he would go to Africa as a missionary. At the time he was ready to go, however, the doors closed to missions. He instead took a position teaching Bible at Davidson College.

"It was the Lord's hand," he told me repeatedly. "He opened the door for my teaching. I wouldn't have missed it for anything."

Mother's Roots

My mother, the daughter of Charles and Elsie Myers, grew up in the manse. Her home was pervaded with the blessings of both Christian faith and Christian activity, so her roots went deep. Dr. Charlie, or "Doc," as her father was affectionately known, was the minister of the First Presbyterian Church in Greensboro, North Carolina. He was a lively and successful pastor, with large and committed vision. Mother once shared with me the depth of his dedication.

"He took out a mortgage on our house," she said, "to make the down payment on the new church building. He would have done anything for the Lord."

Mother watched as her father reached out to many different kinds of people. There was a group of alcoholics whom he be-friended and whom he talked into coming to church. They called themselves, "Doc's Bad Boys," and sat on the front row when they came. Grandfather also went out to the circus when it came to town and invited all the circus people to church. They showed up one Sunday night, saying no minister had ever invited them to come before.

Another nickname my grandfather had was "Multi," which stood for multi-millionaire. Some of his close friends said,

"Multi, you have that same air about you as a man who owns millions."

"That's because there is nothing too good for the Lord," he replied, "Nothing!"

Mother was inspired many times as her dad shared his pulpit with the most influential preachers of his day. He wanted his congregation to have the best.

I was only nine when Grandfather died. It was indicative of his life that in addition to numerous friends, both the local Catholic priest and Jewish rabbi attended his funeral.

Life's Essence

To both my mother and my father, Christianity was not an add-on thing, but was the essence of life; "What life was all about." What I experienced living under their roof was balance, not extreme; love, not harshness. It was probably "caught" as much as "taught."

I witnessed living faith. I saw them read the Bible daily and kneel down together at night to pray. I heard them discuss their tithe and watched as the money went into the plate. I observed them do things quietly behind the scenes, so not to get public acclaim. I also saw them get upset, forgive each other and make up. What they taught me about right and wrong, about godliness and faith, was congruent with their own profound, but unpretentious, spiritual lives. What they imparted to me was this:

"God is real. Live your life for Him. Whatever contribution you do make in life, do it for the Lord."

As long as I can remember, I wanted my life to somehow make a difference for Him.

Although there was much that I absorbed just by being part of the Schenck household, my parents took seriously the scripture,

> Train up a child in the way he should go and when he is
> old he will not depart from it.[1]

I heard Mother quote this verse on numerous occasions.

There was much that they did with the intentionality of laying godly foundations in my life, as well as in my brother's life.

---

[1] Proverbs 22:6

The only part of my "training up" that I remember with distaste, was having to learn the catechism. There I would be, eight-thirty on Sunday morning, seated by Ms. Julia Johnson, answering catechism questions.

"What is the chief end of man?" she read, squinting over the little pink book because the light was so poor.

"To glorify God and enjoy Him forever," I replied in my ten-year-old soprano voice.

"Did I get it right? Can I go now?" I asked, squirming, already knowing that there were four more questions and answers to deal with before my ordeal was over. Patient Ms. Julia!

Bible Stories

Though catechism got an "F" as far as my ratings went, I loved Bible stories. Sunday afternoon was a designated reading time in our house. We had a deal. My parents agreed that they would read as long as I and my brother would keep still. Since my brother and I never tired of hearing Bible stories, we kept very still. Such adventure, suspense, tragedies and miracles.

"Read one more, just one more," we chorused.

The black and white picture of Daniel in the lions' den is still vivid to me. Daniel, standing quite near the lions, looked as serene as a sleeper on a lazy summer day. The lions, on the other hand, were agitated, their surly bodies pacing, their eyes glaring at Daniel. They had, mysteriously, just lost their juicy breakfast. In my mind's eye, I saw those lions leaping towards Daniel, but meeting an invisible force that stopped them in their tracks, forcibly closing their mouths. Daniel, an innocent man, was safe because of the power and watchfulness of God, because God had heard his prayers.

Those stories and illustrations made a deep impression on my life.

Family Prayers

Almost every day, we had family prayers after breakfast. We took turns reading *The Daily Light*. Then Daddy did the praying for all of us. When Daddy prayed, it sounded like he was talking to his closest friend.

One school morning, everything had gone wrong and we were running late. Daddy begin to pray, but looking down at his watch, he realized the time.

"Excuse us, Lord, the school bus is coming. We only have five minutes to get there."

Off we ran for the car. Comfortably, he left off the "Amen."

Forgiveness

Frequently, foundational principles were laid in the midst of my childhood crises. An event that still stands out in my mind occurred when I was six. During the previous week, I had been involved with the other neighborhood children with our own form of "show and tell" time, which included some sexual exploration. Sunday morning came. I was full of shame and uncried tears. My guilt weighed like a heavy ball and chain. The smell of pancakes drifted upstairs, but I had no appetite.

"Daddy, please come up here," I managed to call out.

Striding into my room a few minutes later, my father quickly sensed my "troubledness." Both my eyes and nose ran as I poured out my story. I had "blown it." I felt like "Humpty Dumpty," I could never be put back together again.

"Daddy, I knew better, but I did it anyway," I wailed sorrowfully into his bathrobe.

Holding me close, he explained my need for repentance and what I was to do. He talked about how much God wanted to forgive me.

"The wonderful thing about it," he said smiling, "is that after God forgives you, then He forgets the bad thing that you've done. It is like it never happened. It can work this way because Jesus paid the price for your sin. Are you ready to tell God you are sorry?"

Was I ready! As we knelt down together, I poured out my heart to the Lord. "Please forgive me, God, I don't ever want to do that again. I'm so sorry."

Then my father joined in, speaking in his reassuring way. "Lord, thank You for forgiving Betsy and giving her a new beginning. Thank You for loving her so much."

My guilt and the shame evaporated like mist rising on a sun-filled day. The heaviness lifted. The ball and chain were gone! I was forgiven! Things that I couldn't make right were right again!

As we walked down to breakfast together, I was drenched in that peace that passes all understanding. I was ready for my pancakes.

A Vision

Part of what my parents did for me was simply to take me places where I could experience God for myself, where I could receive. Such was the case one Easter Sunday morning during my early-teen years. At six AM, we packed into our family car and drove over to the lower baseball field behind Davidson College for an early sunrise service. Dew covered my white sandals as we walked across the wet grass to join the gathering crowd. The sky was still filled with quickly-moving gray clouds. Birds were chirping their cheerful morning songs. The cool air had the fresh scent of early spring azaleas mixed with fresh-cut grass. Anticipation dominated my senses. I felt alert and alive. The sweet freshness of the early morning cradled the familiar message of the Easter story.

> Very early in the morning, Mary and the other women went to the tomb. Here they found to their amazement that the great stone blocking the entrance had somehow already been moved out of the way.[1]

The preacher continued, telling the story in his own words.

> They made their way into the cave-like tomb. There, instead of finding the dead body of Jesus, they saw an

[1] Matthew 28:1-7

14

angel. Imagine the shock! No stone and no body. Then to top it all, they saw and heard an angel. "He is not here, He is risen. Go and tell the disciples and Peter. He is risen!"

Wonder and amazement filled me. "Risen!"

"Jesus, You actually came back from the dead, from death to life!"

I wanted to laugh and jump and turn cartwheels. I wanted to shake somebody and say, "It's real. It really happened."

The sun was coming over the horizon, a ball of golden, flaming light. An upheaval of joy rose in dizzying waves that flooded me. I placed my soggy sandals squarely apart to try to keep my balance.

As the service ended, I had an intense yearning to be alone, to savor my thoughts.

"Sure you can walk home by yourself," my mother agreed as I asked her. "It's only a few blocks. We'll have breakfast waiting when you get there."

When I was almost home, all of a sudden, superimposed on my natural surroundings, I saw Jesus, hanging on the cross. He was crying and looking towards me. I did not physically hear words, but I heard them in my spirit.

"I died for you because I love you so much," He said to me. "I love you so much."

My breath came in quick pants. I felt like I was melting. Every part of my being was fluid, undependable. Trembling, the depth of Jesus' love and the truth of His death **for me personally** washed over me, filling me, becoming a reality. This reality was more than a knowing. It saturated me, penetrated me, changed me.

Still weak, I looked again. My natural surroundings had returned. There was Mrs. Fleagle's house and Mrs. Cumming's. There was our hill and my yard. Everything was the same; except for me. I was not the same!

I was quiet at breakfast. It was too soon to share what had happened.

"I think this is going to be a special Easter," Mother commented, bustling around the kitchen.

Deep inside, I agreed. For me, it already had been.

The Powder Keg

As my parents worked on laying a foundation in my life, there was one area that was particularly difficult for them. They were not of the generation that was comfortable discussing sex. There were a few scenes in which my father fled out of the room and my mother closed the door behind him, before answering my pointed questions about the facts of life. My parents, however, never intended to ignore this crucial area. Just at the time the "sap" was beginning to rise in my tender, young life, they placed in my hands a book of sermons by Peter Marshall, entitled *Mr. Jones, Meet the Master*.

"It would be good for you to start with the chapter named, 'The Powder Keg.'"

"Sure," I agreed.

"Now what kind of powder would a preacher be writing about?" I wondered.

In the assigned chapter, Peter Marshall made a graphic comparison between dynamite and sex. He basically said,

"Wow, look out, caution! Don't play with sex. It is as powerful as dynamite. It can blow your life to pieces. Be careful. You're sitting on a powder keg."

"Yes, I agree," I thought to myself, relieved that someone was addressing the powerful, explosive feelings I was experiencing.

"At least maybe I am normal, but I do need to look out for my own dynamite!"

"Well, did you read about the powder keg?" my parents asked in a couple of days.

"Yes, it was good," I answered.

"Good," they sighed, relieved that the job was at least partly taken care of. That was the end of our discussion.

From that time on, I was both reassured and cautioned by what I read and reread in that chapter. With that book, my parents had handed me a comforting but confronting "friend" that helped me through my teenage years.

Commitment

Church, in our family, was simply, "What we did on Sundays." There was never a question of whether or not we were going. Sunday school met at ten, church at eleven. It was settled. We sat about half-way back on the left side in our traditional-looking, but lovely, Presbyterian Church.

It was a warm, spring Sunday my eighth-grade year. I was perched on the wooden seat next to Mother. I was listening as the preacher begin.

"You are called to be 'a living sacrifice, wholly acceptable to God which is your reasonable service.'[1] That's how you can show the Lord that you love Him. That means commitment to serve Him in every part of your life."

Unexplainably, I began to shake inside.

"Every relationship, everything you do should be for Him."

As if in answer to my unspoken question, the preacher's words continued,

"You can't do this on your own, but the Lord will help you if you ask."

I made a decision. I bowed my head.

"Lord, I truly want to be a living sacrifice for You. I promise I will try my best, if You'll be there to help me."

Mother, sitting next to me, didn't seem to notice my shakes, or the tears that were trickling quietly down my cheeks, making my makeup all pasty. No one else was aware of the silent, life-

---

[1] Romans 12:1

17

changing promise I had just made, but I was confident that the Lord had heard my commitment. It was between Him and me.

Mother and I shared an old red hymnal as we stood up to sing. Under my breath I whispered, "Lord, I really mean it."

Over the next years, the Holy Spirit was very faithful to bring that scripture back to me on numerous occasions when I had difficult choices to make.

"You promised to be a 'living sacrifice, holy, acceptable unto God, ...'"

That verse became a standard for me, a cornerstone of values. Though sometimes I failed miserably, I tried hard to keep that promise.

Mother

My mother was so many things to me. Most of them were in some way endearing. With her heavy shock of dark, thick hair, which later turned a glistening white, she was an eye-catcher. Mother brimmed with life, optimism and charisma.

She was "no respecter of persons." She treated the man who sold her mountain apples very much the same way she treated Dr. Layman, a visiting dignitary from Harvard. Her easy warmth and friendliness made people comfortable. With her flair and zest for homemaking, she was an outstanding hostess. Mother loved inviting people to our home.

One thing she didn't tolerate well was pretentiousness, "putting on airs," as she called it. She could smell it as sensitively as hounds smell a fox on a winter hunt. It especially galled her when someone was coming across in a "holier than thou" attitude, being condescending to others.

"Oh pooh, pooh," she would say indignantly, sometimes a little too loud.

Often she would take care of the occasion by quoting one of her favorite limericks:

> When pompous people squelch me with their regal attributes, I chuckle to imagine how they'd look in bathing suits.[1]

Mother's "gracious southern lady" side was definitely there, but it was sometimes overshadowed or upstaged by her "mischievous little-girl side." In the midst of a scenario where she was attempting to express the southern, genteel, slightly-glossed-over-truth, her little-girl side would rise up and "bottom line it," omitting all nuances of grace. She would say exactly what she thought.

---

[1] Author unknown

"Oh dear," she would say to me afterwards, a little chagrined. "I do hope I didn't hurt their feelings. I've got to learn to behave myself."

At eighty-nine, she was still saying this. Most of the time, in her own ineffable way, she got by with it.

Mother loved fun. She loved trips and outings and making an occasion out of anything.

"Now let's see. What are we going to do?"

I could see her imagination swinging into action and before long she would share her idea.

"What do you think?"

Soon we would be off on another little adventure.

Sometimes Mother surprised me. The year my father died, she came to Florida to spend Christmas with us. She was eighty-one at the time. We had spent a long evening playing cards and stayed up much too late.

After giving us all a little lecture about our needing more sleep, she proceeded to initiate a water fight with our college-aged children. She threw the first water and then put out the dare.

"You won't get me wet," she cried, running into her bedroom and slamming the door.

The children hurled down the hall after her. Thirty minutes later, everyone was lying on her floor dissolved in gales of laughter, delightfully and totally soaked. Undaunted, with water dripping from her disheveled hair, Mother questioned the children why they had started this awful water fight so late at night and why they didn't know better. In a funny way, it was the highlight of Christmas; at least it's what we all remember.

Mother was a prolific reader and an astute judge of human nature. She had a large dose of good horse sense. Over the years, I valued and trusted her judgment. It was excellent.

There was one arena, however, with which she was not prepared to deal. There really wasn't any way she could have been. I don't fault her for it, nor do I feel she was somehow responsible for providing my answers.

That arena was my "dark side." While Mother's love and loyalty brought ever so much joy and strength into my life, there was a dark area of gripping fears and dread, of terrible insecurities and self-doubt, that neither she nor I knew how to handle.

"Don't give in to it, don't cater to it, don't give it any place," she would say.

This was good advice as far as it went. I wanted it to work. The fact was, however, that the pain deep within my soul had such an entrenchment that it couldn't be dealt with by being blocked out or ignored. It needed healing. I needed help.

My Dark Side

Perhaps my "dark side" was not dark in the ways you may be thinking. It was not an ugly pile of hidden sins, an area of deep perversion, a force of malicious schemes, or a sinister side held in the clutches of some diabolical, witchcraft spell. Neither was my dark side a foreboding monster waiting to pounce and destroy someone else. My dark side tormented me and me alone. It was filled with night terrors, unrelenting dreads and taunting lies that threatened the very meaning and value of my life. It continuously reminded me that, "I had no right to exist," that "I was a mistake."

For many years, I did not experience my dark side in a way that I could talk about it logically. I did not have a clear mental grasp of its parts or how it all fit together. Furthermore, I was filled with shame for not being able to control or conquer it. Understanding has only come with God's healing, so that now I can put it into a coherent framework. Let me explain.

Fear

As long as I can remember, I lived with the tyrant of Fear. I was as riddled with fear as an old hat used for target practice is riddled with holes. I tried to ignore my fear, bury it, pretend it away, push it aside. I even tried to overcome it with the power of specific scriptures. It would never yield for very long. I despised it. I felt ashamed of it. I dreaded it. I felt victimized by it. When I thought I was about to win over it, it would launch a particularly vicious attack. The fears of my dark side made me feel weak, immature, faithless and sometimes, a little crazy.

My fear had many faces. There was fear of failure, fear of rejection, fear of being left out and fear of losing my "place." However, it was the sweat-drenching fear that I was about to be killed that I hated the most. This fear was most intense at night. My anxiety escalated as the evening shadows began to fall.

As a little girl, I felt dread going up the stairs to my room.

"Step one, two, three."

"Won't somebody come upstairs with me?" I pleaded.

"There is nothing up there. You'll be fine," my parents called back, not wanting to encourage foolish fears.

"Step four, five, six."

I went on alone, feeling more unraveled with every step.

"I'm going to die. It's going to happen this time. I don't want to die. When they come up to tell me good night, it will be too late."

"Step seven, eight, nine, ten."

"I have to go on. I have to face it. I can't turn around. There is no help."

"Step eleven, twelve, thirteen!"

Now I was on the landing.

I was sweaty and cold. Forcing one foot in front of the other, I entered my room.

"Where will it come from, the dreaded thing that is about to kill me. Will it be in the closet, or under the bed? Is it planning to wait until I go to sleep and then murder me before I know what is happening?"

Quickly, I got ready for bed. I kept my pajamas in the drawer so I didn't have to open the closet. I lay down in the bed stiffly, waiting, waiting, waiting ...

Many nights I heard my parents come up for bed before I could go to sleep. Even then I would have bad dreams, or be startled, wide awake, when something went "bump" in the night.

This torturous scenario repeated itself over and over again, night after night, week after week, year after year after year. Sometimes it was a little better; sometimes a little worse. The dread was never further away than the darkness.

With morning's light I would take heart.

"Surely I will outgrow this," I hoped against hope. I didn't.

As I grew older, the shame that I couldn't overcome such "childish ways" only escalated.

"God, how can I say that I trust You and still go into a frozen sweat if the door blows open?"

I read every self-help book I could find, Christian and otherwise. I tried many strategies, all to no avail. I felt like a child, trying desperately to grow up, but who had a malfunctioning pituitary gland. An essential key was missing. I felt hopelessly stuck in this nightmare. It was wretched, infuriating, loathsome to me; a source of self-hate. I was shackled.

"How do you think you are going to serve the Lord in any significant way when you can't even get through the night without fear?" a voice from deep inside ridiculed me. "What kind of testimony is that, especially after walking with Him all these years?"

I always thought the voice was myself speaking.

"Lord," I screamed in exasperation. "Why don't You do something? Why don't You fix me? I **don't know how to fix myself**!"

His only answer seemed to be silence.

"Doesn't He care?" I wondered.

In my frustration, I began to blame Him. I wanted to serve God, but I was angry with Him, furious. I was in a "double bind."

"Why should I do something for You, God, when You won't even help me?"

In the midst of my fears, my dilemma, my double bind; there was a searching question which defied all explanat- ion.

"Where had this relentless fear of death come from, this dreadful sense that I am about to be killed? What was its source?"

I knew that my life had never been threatened in Davidson, my safe, little community, full of so many friends.

24

"Had something happened earlier, before Davidson and my home?"

I had no way of knowing the answer.

My Bogeymen

During my teen years, shameful thoughts and haunting questions were added to my problem of fear. They begin to emerge like bogeymen, coming uninvited, up out of the basement of my life into my living room. With my increased awareness of sexuality, the issues underlying my adoption forced themselves to the surface.

"Why was I given up? Why was I not wanted? Was my life the result of rape or incest?

Intensifying the pain of my identity crisis was the fact that at the very time I was trying so hard to be sexually pure, I had to face a hard reality: the very premise of my life had probably been based on illicit sex. Put simply, my life was the result of something I couldn't respect. I felt as if my life had a false premise.

One bogeyman said, "If those people had been living up to your standards, you wouldn't even be here."

No Right to Exist

One spring day, I was walking home from high school. The honeysuckle had popped out along the path and the birds were chirping away in the trees. In spite of the brightness of the day, I felt a dark, cold shadow come over my life. I was having a series of excruciatingly painful thoughts.

"Maybe the me that is walking home is **not supposed** to be here. Maybe where I am leaving these tracks in this red dirt, there were never supposed to be any tracks. Maybe I am **not supposed** to exist. Do I have a **right** to be breathing the air, eating the food, taking my little measure from the earth? If I don't have a right to exist, if I was never supposed to have been born, then there couldn't be any plan or purpose for my life. I am an intruder, an unwelcome guest, who somehow was able to slip in."

25

For the first time, all of the logical implications of my illegitimate birth pounded me full force. The sweat of despair drenched my body and the green-plaid dress I was wearing. I was drained.

In that instant, I accepted as truth the devastating lie, the lie that came to have a stranglehold on my life, the lie that said,

"I have no right to exist."

Suddenly, I felt hurled light years away from everything that had given my life meaning and value: from years of parental love, from my cherished friends and community, from my vision of Jesus, so intimately expressing the depth of His love for me, from my promised commitment to live for Him. I felt wrenched away from all of these, severed, disconnected, alone.

"I have no right to exist," I grimaced. I just wanted to die.

Who could I tell? Who would want to know? Who would understand? What the Bible said about "being chosen from the foundation of the world" couldn't possibly apply to people who were born by "accident," people who "slipped in." I couldn't risk speaking to anyone about this issue, asking them about it. Besides, I already knew the answer.

I never felt so alone. The specialness, the confidence, the sense of purpose and destiny I had believed so strongly about myself as a child, all were destroyed, gone, in a moment of time.

The Octopus

As I tried to face my life-shattering conclusion, it never occurred to me that my painful identity issue might be common for other adopted children. I thought I was unique and that these problems were uniquely mine. But I am not unique, at least, not in this way.

Besides adoption, there are many reasons that can cause a person to feel he has **no right to exist.** Almost any form of physical or emotional abandonment, abuse, extreme criticism, or being a scapegoat, can lead a person to this same tormenting conclusion.

Feeling/believing that one has **no right to exist** is much more than a psychological or philosophical concept. It is a reality with many powerful, everyday implications. It affects how one gets up in the morning, how one relates to others and what one dreams of accomplishing. In short, it strongly effects one's sense of purpose and destiny. It is like an octopus whose grasping tentacles hold captive almost every part of his victim's life.

That day, walking home from high school, I accepted the deadly axiom, **"I have no right to exist."** This axiom led to three grim corollaries, three interconnecting lies which almost destroyed my life.

"I am a Mistake"

The first corollary was the conclusion that, **"I am a mistake."**

This is the core belief that underlies shame: wretched, accusing, belittling shame. Shame caused me not to want to look at people, or life, straight in the eye. How could I look straight ahead with my head bowed? Shame is different from guilt. Whereas guilt says, "I have **done** something wrong," shame says, "I **am** wrong." The problem is me, **"I am a mistake."**

This belief kept me tied to the treadmill of striving; striving to prove to myself and to others that I **did** have value, that I was **not** a mistake.

But there was never enough proof! "Work, work, work. Try, try, try, push, push, push! Now, before you go to bed to rest, try a little harder!"

I also constantly apologized. I felt like a burden, an imposition. "I don't have any rights here, I am a mistake."

"Oh, excuse me. Excuse me. Excuse me for breathing your air!"

I was trapped in what we now call the ***"Shame-Fear-Control Dynamic."***[1] It can take many forms, but one common form is this:

---

[1] God has showed us much more about the ***Shame-Fear-Control Stronghold*** and how to minister to it. We have devel-

27

"I am bad." (*Shame*)

"I am afraid that someone will find out how bad I really am." (*Fear*)

"I will control things (myself and others) so that no one will ever find out (how bad I really am)." (*Control*)

The foreboding fear and the resulting control I experienced was more a mode of operation than a conscious awareness. I lived on guard, so that people wouldn't see the "real me" and be disappointed. This fear consumed vast amounts of my energy. There were very few times when I could relax and rest.

"I am Unworthy"

A second corollary coming out of my axiom that "I have no right to exist," was the belief, "**I am unworthy**."

"Unworthy of what?" you might ask.

"Anything. Everything."

On any scale, I deserved to be at the bottom. If everyone else is supposed to be here in this world, but I am not, then that automatically makes "everyone else" more valuable than me. My "unworthiness" was an established fact.

The belief that I was so much less valuable than others led me to give up my own God-given rights many times: rights to my time, my opinions, my preferences, my integrity. It even included rights that made life richer for me, such as travel and classical music.

I was not being victimized by someone else. I was being victimized by my "dark side." I was in bondage to the lies I believed about myself. As a result, I was "selling out" my own life, being passively accommodating; a slave in invisible chains.

oped a two-tape plus handouts teaching/ministry resource to help others obtain freedom from this threefold tyrant. This resource is available from our ministry, Proclaiming His Word Ministries. For information on how to contact us, please see "About the Author" at the end of this book.

There is always a place and a time for kindness, for unselfishness and for Godly submission, but I was living way out of balance.[1]

"I don't Belong"

A person who doesn't have a right to exist doesn't feel that he has **any place** that he really fits or belongs. This was true for me. This led to the third corollary that I accepted without question, **"I don't belong."**

Other than with my parents, I had no place I felt I could just be myself and feel completely accepted. I always felt on the outside, even when I was the chosen leader, the president, the organizer. Being the leader was like being an "inside-outsider."

When I was able to achieve a little sense of belonging, I would desperately try to protect it. I would fight, connive, control and even compromise my values, to retain it. I just wanted to belong!

Always operating within me was the feeling of "impending loss," that I was about to lose whatever tenuous place of belonging I temporarily had.

Any action that even hinted of conflict or controversy threatened my sense of belonging. I avoided both of these fiercely. Disagreement or anger felt too much like rejection, like I was losing my place of "belonging" with the other person.

"You're out of here, you don't belong," my gut would say when someone disagreed with me. Often, I was not able to differentiate between issues of discussion and issues of relationship.

Even when I was actually being quite well received, my dark side would lie to me, telling me that "I didn't belong." Because I didn't have a right to exist, I would believe all of its freedom-stealing, life-crushing lies. They seemed so right, so normal. They were my reality. They were "just the way things were."

My life felt like a portrait painted by several artists who had not consulted with each other. The theme, the mood, the colors of

[1] Hostility always comes out of this pattern, whether it is expressed explicitly or undercover.

what each one created, clashed disjointedly with the others. One painted the happy "Davidson Betsy," bubbling with the love of life. Another brought forth the "Struggling Betsy," believing she had no "right to exist." A third artist portrayed a "Spiritually-Ambivalent Betsy," trying to trust a God who wasn't healing her. The canvas was a strange configuration of discord. All of these "Betsys" were trying to live together inside of one skin; "my" skin!

College

In the fall of 1959, I covered over my "dark side" with my bright-red jumper and headed for Atlanta to begin college at Agnes Scott, a small Christian liberal arts college. I had fallen in love with this college when I first saw it in *A Man Called Peter*, a movie about the lives of Peter and Catherine Marshall. It was enough like Davidson to feel familiar and comfortable. There stood the college with all its tall, stately, Gothic buildings, complete with pigeons and gracious magnolias, looking remarkably like something out of the middle ages. A great place to study Chaucer's *Canterbury English Tales*!

I was bursting to get going. The stimulation of new friends, studies and a new city to explore were all tonic for my soul. I stayed up late, ate my desserts before my vegetables and even kissed somebody on a first date. New freedoms!

In college, the tormenting fears of my dark side were immediately decreased. The scene had changed. There were nearly a thousand girls living within a few square blocks. I felt the protection of numbers. My fears went underground. They only emerged when I was in a situation that required me to face the darkness, alone. I tried to gather my "disjointed" self into "one" self and make a new beginning.

"Maybe here, I can defeat my dark side."

The first week was a rush of smiling faces, finding my way to classes, going in white gloves to a tea at the president's home and finding out that I had to "sign out" at the dean's office to go across the street to get a hamburger. After all, I was at an "all girls" school on the edge of a big city and the administration felt an obligation to keep up with each one of us.

Best Score

The first Friday afternoon all of us freshman were required to come to the gym in groups of 25, sporting our modest, new, gray gym uniforms. We were to be "put through" the freshman Strength and Agility test. Mother style, I "pooh poohed" it.

31

"Maybe we've gone the wrong direction and we're really here to join the Marines," I quipped.

Push ups, running, crawling over and under objects; all were tests for speed. I felt sorry for the heavier girls who were painfully out of breath.

Later that afternoon, I heard the news. I had made the best score in our freshman class!

Suddenly, other girls were coming up to me admiringly.

"Hey, you're Betsy, aren't you. That was pretty good this afternoon," said an attractive, blond-headed girl named Lynn. Others waved and smiled.

"Dark side, you're losing out," I said to myself with new confidence. "See, I'm already finding my place. I do belong!"

Elected

"You won, you won, you won!" It was late October and the reds and golds of the campus trees had announced fall. Several girls, out of breath, came flying into my dorm room in Rebecca Scott Hall.

"You and Lynn were elected from our dorm to serve on the Judicial Board of Student Government. We just read it over in the post office where the elections are posted. Isn't that great!"

Face glowing, I received their congratulations. I could hardly believe it. I pushed my dark side further away from me.

Accepted

That fall, I learned several things about myself. One was that people liked me. Not just the people I had grown up with, but new people, girls my own age.

"I wonder what they are seeing that they like?"

I also found that I had great satisfaction helping other girls with their problems.

"You are so easy to talk to," they would say.

It seemed to me that the right words just came easily when it was my turn to talk.

In this soil, my roots of belonging were beginning to grow.

At the same time, I also realized that my dark side was still there, lurking uncannily in the background like a dark shadow. Once again, I was in a place of leadership, but I still felt undeserving, unworthy. Once again, I began to strive to prove my worth.

"You are still an 'inside-outsider,'" my dark side would remind me.

James

The summer after my freshman year I met James. We were both working at Montreat, North Carolina, a long-time conference center for Presbyterians. There was an immediate spark. James and I roamed the lovely mountainsides, threw rocks into Lake Susan and talked about the great themes of life.

We had much in common. Both of our fathers were Presbyterian ministers. Mine taught Bible; his dad had spent many years as a pastor. James was majoring in English with a minor in philosophy. I was majoring in philosophy with a minor in English. A year ahead of me, he had already started reading Dostoyesky. I was impressed.

James starred in the world of ideas, a world that I loved. Our conversations were never finished. There was always more and he was always a jump ahead of me in his understanding, bringing new insight into our discussions. I was intrigued.

There was also a pervasive sweetness about him, a gentle sensitivity. I liked the way he treated me. I liked his serious eyes and his good looks.

"I better keep a lid on the Powder Keg," I thought, cautioning myself.

I started missing James before the summer was even over, just knowing that we were going to be separated.

"I think I love you," he whispered, the night before we parted.

"Yes, me too. I mean, I think I love you too," I said.

I wrote a voluminous letter before I left, just so he wouldn't miss me too much. James was going to Davidson College where his father and brother had both gone before him and where my dad was still teaching. Yes, we did have lots in common.

College

My college years were passing quickly. There were many bright spots. My relationship with James continued to flourish. I had a big picture of him beside my bed and a wallet-size one I could look at any time. I enjoyed my classes, except for freshman biology, where all of the little wiggly things I was supposed to identify looked the same to me under the microscope.

"Now, show me again," I asked Nancy Rose, who obviously could see the difference. "How do you tell them apart?"

I made several close friends, Nancy included. Each year, I served on the Judicial Board. Each year was more rewarding.

During my first two years, I got a jump on my dark side. I learned that I could tell my dark side to "Shut up." Perhaps this was not very ladylike for a southern woman, but it responded to my new found force. "Shut up," I said, practicing out loud. "Shut up, shut up, shut up. I'm tired of listening to you. Shut up and leave me alone."

I discovered that "Shut up" worked on many occasions. For almost three years it worked well. I was gaining on it, heading, I thought, for victory.

Return of My Dark Side

Spring of my junior year, my dark side came out fighting. It was tired of being kicked around and must have been gathering venom. The test came on unsuspecting ground.

I had been nominated to run for President of the Student Body. There were several other excellent candidates. Excited, I was poised to give it my best effort.

"You are not qualified," the old voice thundered in my head. "You'll just get up there in front of a thousand girls and make a fool of yourself. You'll be sorry. The truth about you will be exposed. Remember, you are 'nothing but a mistake, nothing but a mistake, nothing but a mistake, nothing but a mistake!'"

This refrain pelted my mind like baseball-size hail. My head throbbed.

"But I've done well," I insisted. "I want to give it a try."

"You're crazy," it countered, opening both barrels of ammunition. "You've fooled them this far. You should stop while you're ahead! Remember, you don't have a right to exist! How dare you try to run for such an office? You shouldn't even be here!"

The barrage was sudden and unexpected. The old feelings covered me like a pile of musty, outgrown, old overcoats, pressing me down, constricting me with the weight of the past. The words rang out sharply, stinging, blasting away at my new found, fragile confidence. All of my "Shut ups" were mute, muzzled. I could find no confrontive words to keep up the fight.

Weary and unhealed, head still pounding, I yielded, bowing to the hated lies. In the lateness of the star-strewn spring night, I walked slowly over to the old campus post office and scratched my name off the list of candidates. My defeat had already taken place! It was greater than the outcome of any election.

The next year was bitter sweet. The girl who won the election was an excellent leader, one our class was proud of. There were days when I thought with regret of what might have been.

College years provided more than the usual accolades, especially for someone who had "no right to exist." Judicial Board, president of a freshman dorm, Who's Who in American Colleges and Universities. Academically and socially, I had been a "success." I appeared to others, and even to myself, to have so much promise; and yet I knew that my dark side could erupt without warning, just as it had that defeating, spring night.

I knew that my "Shut up" didn't always work. Saying "Shut up" was not the same as being healed.

I was not about to give up on life, however. Still determined, I was preparing to follow my dream. I was planning a wedding!

Marriage

Whereas many of my classmates were preparing for graduate school and careers, my deepest desire was to establish a happy home. In James, I was sure I had found the right man to make it work. We had dated for three years. Our love blossomed out into many dimensions, many interests and commonalities. Our commitment and our passion for each other grew. I was tired of sitting on the lid of my "Powder Keg!"

At five o'clock in the afternoon on a sweltering-hot July Saturday, I was ready. I was in the back of the Davidson College Presbyterian Church, dressed in ivory ruffles and fluffles, waiting to walk down the long aisle, waiting to say my vows of commitment.

I looked out at my church, the church I had attended for as long as I could remember. There were all of my friends. There was the pew where I had made my secret commitment to Jesus. There was the cross, hanging in front where it had always hung.

My mother, looking beautiful in her long, blue-voile dress, had already been seated. The bridesmaids, in yellow chiffon, carrying yellow and white daises, were arranged between the handsome groomsmen, including my brother.

My Daddy, who moments before had hurried back to the bride's dressing room to give me a final kiss, appeared at the front of the church, in full command of the situation. He was going to marry us.

James stood next to him, beaming down the white-ribboned aisle at me.

Everything was just right. I was ready. As I moved forward to the glorious strains of the organ music, I felt like I was floating; floating into a life of dedicated commitment, floating into a new future of hope, floating into the arms of my soon-to-be-lover for life.

"I will," I promised, with everything within me.

"I will," James said, with tender steadiness.

I loved his voice, everything about him.

"I now pronounce you man and wife. You may kiss the bride," my father said.

In the middle of the kiss, I could hear my friend Evelyn crying as she sat on the front row.

We sprang joyously back down the aisle, happy to be one.

James and I moved to Richmond, Virginia, with as many wedding presents as we could carry. While James attended graduate school, I taught seventh grade. I was extremely proud of being the bread winner, coming home with a paycheck. My pride and my career, however, were both short lived!

Pregnant

In November, we had gone to Washington to protest the Viet Nam War. Driving back, I felt extremely sick. We surmised that I must have eaten something that disagreed, or maybe I was just too tired.

Through that night and next day, the violent stomach virus took its toll. By the weekend I was hospitalized for dehydration.

Smiling, the doctor said, "Before I put you on medication, I would like to run a pregnancy test."

"Just like a doctor," I thought skeptically, "putting you through a bunch of expensive tests that you don't need."

The results of the pregnancy test were positive.

"Your stomach virus," he announced smiling, "is a baby!"

"A baby? A baby?" There was a new life inside of me and I didn't even know it! My first child. Unbelievable. "I am going to have a baby! We are going to have a baby."

Not only was I a new wife, I was going to be a new mother. My life whirled around me with dizzying disorientation.

I was vomiting too much to go back to work. I went to the bathroom so often that I decided to just leave the toilet seat up. In between upheavals, I arranged and rearranged our green couch, geranium lamps and the old coffee table that had come from James's home. Our apartment was attractive and inviting.

"It's going to be all right, Honey," James said several times, knowing that I was worried about our finances.

Predictably, as always when the chips were down, my dark side chimed in.

"You're in a mess and its your fault. You don't look good, you don't smell good and you're not bringing home a pay check. You're even getting fat."

I agreed that I was a pretty awful sight. It all seemed true. I didn't even have the heart to say, "Shut up." It was a rough beginning.

Our parents were more than happy to help us financially. They were very supportive and only said positive things about our having a baby.

"If it's a boy, I would like to name him for you," I told James as the time grew nearer. He liked the idea too.

As the time approached, I went by to see a wonderful, motherly black woman, Mildred, who was going to help me for the first two weeks after our baby was born.

"I'm so glad you're coming," I confessed. "I'm really not sure I know what to do."

"Don't you worry about a thing, Honey," she said. "When it comes to babies, the directions 'comes' with the package."

James
A few weeks later towards the end of July, our eight-pound son, James Jr., discovered America.

I examined him over and over with amazement. All the parts were there. Everything worked. Repeatedly, I tiptoed in to make sure he was breathing. Even though my sore bottom testified to the fact that I had just had a baby, it was still hard to believe this tiny, perfect human being had come out of my womb.

He began to smile and "coo," and I giggled back. I picked him up and held him to my breast to nurse. Mildred was right about the directions. I knew how to be a mother!

That fall, our parents continued to help us financially so that I could stay home and begin to raise little James. We moved into married-student housing, a big U-shaped building, known affectionately as "The Fertile Crescent." I watched our baby and took in ironing to help ends meet.

Graduate School

Meanwhile, graduate school began with a vengeance and my student-husband worked voraciously, completing unending assignments and typing papers.

"It will all be over next spring," I reminded myself on lonely evenings. I tried to remember what it was we had talked about for such long hours. Sometimes it seemed hard to find anything to say.

James did so well that the following spring he was awarded a post-graduate fellowship. His dream was to study for a year under a scholar, Dr. Schweizer, in Zurich, Switzerland.

Pregnant

Two weeks before our flight abroad, I woke up vomiting. This time, I knew it wasn't a virus!

Checking me out, our family doctor reassuringly said, "Don't worry, there have been lots of babies born in Switzerland!"

I opened our steamer trunk one last time and put in my maternity clothes, as well as the baby clothes James Jr. had just outgrown. Things were happening almost too fast for me. Just two years earlier, I had been graduating from college myself. Now, I was married, had a baby, was pregnant again and about to go to Switzerland!

Switzerland

Zurich, well known for its banks with unnumbered bank accounts, is a fascinating old city. It is located on a large lake and has two historic, gothic cathedrals, the Fraumunster and the Grossmunster, which stand like sentinels guarding the city.

After flying to Zurich, James and I and baby James moved into the International House for foreign students, located a few blocks from the lake. We were the only Americans and I was the only woman in the apartment house. Within a day we found the Salvation Army and purchased our needed furnishings: a bed, a crib, a couch, a little table and some lamps. Not having a car, we rode on top of our "new" furniture as the truck made its way back to Waldistrasse #5.

James had work to do. Preparing to take all of his classes in German, he left for two months to attend a "beefed-up" language school in Germany. It was an essential part of his preparation.

Fear Returns

I was left alone. I had a strange city to navigate, a new language to conquer and most disconcerting of all, I was still vomiting. Fainting in the local grocery store, I didn't yet know enough German to explain that I was pregnant to the kind people gathered around me.

The days and nights were long without my husband. For the first time since before college, I was left alone to face the darkness.

"I'm fine," I exhorted myself, beginning about five PM the day he left. I sang little James to sleep and then turned on the radio. Later I read some of my favorite scriptures and then reread a letter from home.

> Daddy and I are proud of you. You have a lot of responsibility now taking care of a family, but we know you can do it. We know you will be fine. Daddy is going to retire at the end of next college year and we will come to see you. By that time the new baby will be six months old. Can you believe it? Can hardly wait to see

you. It always helps to have something to look forward to! Do write and let us know if you need anything. We can send it airmail if necessary. Well, I want to get this in the mail. It is frustrating to know that it will take five days before it reaches you. Never forget how much we love you. Special love, Mother.

As I was reading, there was a crash outside of my front door; a crash and then silence. Then the wretched voice inside of me began to speak.

"You're all alone. Nobody knows you. Nobody will miss you. Nobody will look for you. Nobody will find you!"

The hair on my arms stood straight up. I felt like something had hold of my throat. I heard footsteps outside of my door, then silence. The only telephone was on the third floor of our apartment house, out in the hall.

"I can't possibly call for help. I might not make it to the phone. Who would I call? Would I tell the police, 'There are footsteps outside my door?'" That sounded ridiculous, even to me. "No, I should stay where I am and do all that I can to keep my baby safe."

Silence, the fullness of uncomfortable silence. "Who am I sharing it with? Who is on the other side of my door?"

"Sing a hymn, pray, **do something** to break the foreboding quietness."

The curtains blew open reminding me that my window was open onto the street.

"Get it closed quickly. Who else has seen that it is open? Will it lock? Yes, thank goodness!"

"Oh, Mother, I'm not fine. I'm terrified. I don't know if I'll ever see you again. I'm afraid I'm going to be killed. I don't know what will happen to my baby. I don't know what to do to protect myself. I'm afraid to go to bed. I feel too vulnerable lying down. Oh, Mother, I wish you weren't so impossibly far away."

I forced myself to go check on James and to close his window too, even though the June air was warm and heavy.

"Nobody will ever know," the chilling voice began again.

"Shut up," I said in my mind, my frozen voice refusing to speak out loud. "Why does this have to happen to me, why?"

The night moved in slow-paced increments, like an elderly person learning to walk on a walker. With the windows closed, the stale odors of old carpet and sour creosote from the wood stove filled the room.

Every muscle on tense alert, I sat straight up in a chair facing the door. At least I wouldn't be surprised.

The night dragged on. I don't know how much I slept. I felt cold and stiff when the baby's happy sounds alerted me that it was day.

Some nights I was able to sleep; others, I watched and waited and listened. When James came back from Germany, I wanted to tell him, but shame of my fear caused me to minimize my experiences.

"You look so tired," he said, smoothing my hair back away from my face.

"I am," I replied, but I couldn't explain.

There is a depth of defeat that paralyzes hope, that stifles the human soul from trying to reach out for what's needed. It resigns itself to just surviving, to just getting through the next day. Such resignation was mine that first summer.

"Is my dark side going to win for the rest of my life?"

Who am I?
During the long days, I begin to discover something even more unsettling about myself. I realized that in this distant land, adrift from my family setting and my southern culture, without relatives or friends to "please," I didn't really know who I was. I had spent so much of my time and energy pleasing other people that without them, I felt lost. I didn't quite know what to do

with myself. Even my husband, who might have been a candidate for "pleasing," was away.

"There has to be a 'me' inside who knows **who I am and what I want**," I cried out loud, "but how do I find her?"

"You **can't** find her because she has **no right to exist**," my despicable dark side said, as if it were an eternally settled matter.

"No, no, no," I screamed back. "I don't know how, but I will find her."

That fall, James went to classes at the University of Zurich, while I looked after our toddler, went to natural childbirth classes and took long walks by the lake to get in good shape.

"We're going to be fine," I reassured my growing baby. "I can't wait to see you."

Lewis

In February, our wonderful new son arrived. I was delighted to have two little boys. Proudly, we named him Lewis Schenck after my father.

Lewis was sturdy, took long naps and was marvelously good natured. He was a delight. I felt a fresh sense of purpose as I created a little bed for him out of our dresser drawer. He grew so quickly that we had to get a second crib long before we had planned.

Lewis was born in a hospital where no one spoke English. I had learned German rapidly. The only problem was trying to figure out where to use my hospital vocabulary. There were not a lot of social occasions where it was appropriate to say, "Please hand me the bed pan!"

As promised, my parents came the next summer. Daddy took walks by the lake with little James and proudly helped to feed his new namesake.

"He is really something," he said again and again, looking at me like I had accomplished a miracle. My parents commented on every possible positive about our funny makeshift apartment. "We're proud of you, Betsy. You're making a good home."

The normality and easy companionship of their visit gave me fuel to continue on.

"Good-bye, Sugar," my father said. "Remember that the Lord is always with you. You are never alone."

I think they knew how much I was struggling.

After they left, my loneliness was intensified. James and I made a hard decision. He wanted to stay more years and do an advanced degree at the University. I didn't want to stay, but also didn't want to cheat him out of his dreams. I thought about our wedding vows, my commitment to stay with him and be supportive under every kind of condition. I wanted to do my best, but at the same time, I didn't look forward to staying longer in Europe.

Trouble

During the four years we were in Europe, not only was I having an identity crisis, but also our marriage was deteriorating. What was happening? It's hard to describe. Was James secretly a terrible person? No. Was I? No.

Nevertheless, neither one of us had dealt with our dark sides. Serious lacks in both of us began to unravel our bonds of promise. Our problems were more than the fact that he was engrossed in work and I was raising small children.

As James sought to deal with his anger over issues from his past and identity issues within himself, he went through long, sobering times of depression. Living in Europe, we lacked some of the natural supports and safeguards that might have helped undergird our marriage.

Meanwhile, I took it personally. I felt rejection and failure because my love wasn't enough to make everything all right for him, for us. I carried a false responsibility for making him happy. I was afraid of the angry side of him and was still unable to cope with conflict.

For me, the issue of not "having a right to exist" had done much to erode my once-strong faith. Also, as I focused on college and marriage, my faith had slipped into neutral. I did not know where I stood with God. In addition, James and I were never able to establish a joint spiritual life together in the Word or in prayer, so we lacked this major source of godly "marital glue." Our emotional and spiritual separation deepened. I certainly didn't hate James, but for a long time I had felt the loneliness of an unbreachable gulf between us.

Heartbreak

Our attempts at getting help were neutral, or worse. My first pastoral counselor was also a Jungian dream analyst. That help was short-lived.

The second one, picked by James after we came back to the States, was a needy man himself. After several counseling sessions, he invited me to have a "rendezvous" with him.

Still desperate, we tried once more. The third counselor suggested that we might try a trial separation. This was a major mistake. Although I chose into this of my own volition, my despair and confusion left me an easy target for the enemy's schemes.

I was thirty years old and headed for divorce. I believed that my life was over. I had failed in the things that mattered most: having a godly home with a satisfied husband and secure children.

"How could anything that looked so gloriously right, end in such miserable defeat? How could my life, apparently so successful, not have the right ingredients to hold a marriage together? How could the very thing that I wanted to succeed in the most, still end up failing?"

My marriage had only lasted seven years.

Divorce blew on the flames of my dark side.

"See, I told you so. You really are a bad person. This proves it."

Running

No one in my family had ever been divorced. Now I was disgracing them. I hurt for them as well as for myself. There were times I wanted to blurt out,

"Look, I hate this as much as you do. I don't understand it any better than you do. All I know is that I have this crazy side of myself that says, 'I'm no good,' and that, 'I shouldn't even be here.' It says that, 'I am a mistake,' and, 'I'll never belong.' I keep trying, but I always lose. All I know is that **I am broken** and I don't know what to do or where to go to get fixed!"

Instead, I said nothing. I tried to avoid those people who had once believed in me.

I looked around at what had been our attractive living room. Now there were large empty spaces where once a couch, a chair and a grandfather clock had stood. The room's emptiness seemed the outward expression of the gaping holes I felt in my own life.

Sometimes there were midnight wishes that I could just end it all. At times, I wondered if my decision to get a divorce was a tragic mistake.

I grieved for myself, for my children, even for James, for what might have been.

Our sons' heartache added to my own. Guilt. These wonderful little boys, only five and six, were so full of life, so loving and tender, so trusting. They didn't deserve this.

"I miss my daddy," Lewis said at bed time. "I want Daddy to read me a story. Then I can go to sleep."

Explanations didn't take the pain away, theirs or mine. Even reassurance that "it wasn't their fault" was small comfort to them in the face of life shattering trauma.

Somewhere along the way, I heard the expression, "God hates divorce." He doesn't hate divorced people, just "divorce." The reason soon became plain; so many lives are crushed. Like most divorces, ours left a path of grief-strewn people: parents, close friends, business contacts, acquaintances. Our lives touched a wider sphere than we had realized.

In the midst of my anguish was the fact that I didn't know where I stood with God. I knew that God hated divorce and that I had totally failed Him. Ashamed, feeling cut off, I avoided Him as well. As my marriage crumbled, so did my life's dream that I would ever be able to serve Him, that He would let me do something for Him that would make a difference.

"What good were all those years of godly training now?" I wondered.

At times, I read the Psalms and questioned.

> Because he (David) has loved Me, therefore I will deliver him; I will set him securely on high, because he has known my name; He will call on Me and I will answer him; I will be with him in trouble; I will rescue him and honor him; with long life I will satisfy him and let him behold My salvation.[1]

"Lord, You delivered David in the time of His trouble. What about me?"

All I heard was my dark side saying, "You don't deserve a second chance."

"It's true," I agreed, turning and walking away from God.

God's Protection

God, however, had neither rejected me nor given up on me. Even when we are unfaithful to God, He is faithful to us![2] He did a lot of special things for me during my "running away" years. I knew it was Him. He provided money for me to secure my home, opened up a job for me at the community college in

[1] Psalms 91:14-15 NAS
[2] II Timothy 2:13

the middle of a year-long hiring freeze and miraculously kept my car together. He protected me from getting hooked when I dabbled in psychic and occult pathways.

He also protected me from marrying on the rebound. When one comes out of a broken relationship, it is easy to be attracted to people who provide the major thing that was missing in the former relationship. It's a setup and at first, I fell for it. The man I began dating had those elusive "missing qualities," but he also had serious shortcomings.

"Don't do it," God's still, small voice whispered. "You know you don't have any peace."

I broke off the relationship.

Unexplained

I ran from God for several years and knew that I was running. I was quite a mess and I knew that too. At the same time, in the midst of myself was a relentless desire to serve Him.

"Go away foolish desire. You don't fit. Don't you know I've blown it? Stop tormenting me. The window of opportunity for me is shut."

The same week I was preaching this message so ardently to myself, I made an appointment to have an interview at a well-respected Presbyterian Seminary in Decatur, Georgia. Could I still be trained for the ministry?

The interview confirmed that seminary was not for now, but Dr. Ben Cline gave me a key.

"As a divorced person, there are some doors that will be closed to you," he said, "but not all doors. You must wait and see what God opens."

Hidden in his statement was a seed that gave hope. **He believed** that God could still use me.

As I began to turn again to scripture, I realized that God had called out to Israel in her darkest hour to come back to Him. God continued to love her even in her unfaithfulness.

Therefore also now, says the Lord, turn and keep on coming to Me with all your heart, with fasting, with weeping and with mourning until every hindrance is removed and the broken fellowship is restored. Rend your hearts and not your garments and return to the Lord your God, for He is gracious and merciful, slow to anger and abounding in loving-kindness and He revokes His sentences of evil (when His conditions are met).[1]

"Lord, I don't care what my dark side says. I know You still love me. I'm tired of running. I'm coming back. Will You give me another chance?"

[1] Joel 2:12-13, AMP

Singleness

My life started to come back together, but the pieces didn't re-assemble easily. They were more like the toy one tries to put together at the last minute on Christmas Eve, that defies directions. Even with the Lord's help, it took time.

Misfit

Gradually, I grew accustomed to the life of being a single parent. As a single parent, feeling like a misfit becomes the norm. One doesn't belong to the world of marrieds, or to the world of singles.

One evening I got a double whammy. At the Cub Scout meeting, each set of parents stood up proudly as their son received his badges. I hadn't anticipated having to take part. I was the only single parent there. Self-consciously, I felt that peculiar embarrassment, that gray shame. My face flushed. There were not two parents, but only one of me to stand on behalf of my son. Hurting for both of us, I wondered if he noticed, if he hurt too.

A few hours later that same evening, as the scout trauma faded and the baby-sitter arrived, I went out on a "double date" to get some coffee. Sitting there with three singles, in a smoky cafe filled with graduate students, I felt like the clock of my life was somehow turning backwards. I didn't feel "cute." I didn't feel like "date bait."

As the others spoke excitedly about the great events coming up over spring break, I was preoccupied. I was wondering to myself whether or not my children had clean socks and underwear for school the next day. I was a Mom. I didn't fit with the singles either. When I got home, I curled up in the big, yellow bean bag chair and cried. Our fluffy terrier came over and licked my hands and face until I finally ran out of tears.

Choosing Singleness

My life as a misfit also had some humorous moments. On another occasion, a fellow graduate student unexpectedly came by to see me. As he rode up in our driveway on his motorcycle, I realized too late that I had not told him about my children. He stopped and surveyed the situation. There I was smiling and waving, accompanied by my two sons and their four friends, two mother dogs and five puppies. The scene was too much. The expression on his face was good material for the *Best Home Videos* program. Looking pale, "Easy Rider" turned his motorcycle around and rode away into his life of freedom.

It didn't really hurt. I was putting my life back together. I had been single for three years and I was over the worst. I made a firm decision not to remarry. For me, singleness was best. My life was full and complicated enough.

I was teaching, directing a para-professional counseling program, going to graduate school and trying to be a decent Mom. It was all I could handle. I remember looking at myself in the mirror while wearing my hair curlers and wondering if I were going to bed or getting up! Let this decision be settled. I'll be safe and single. After all, there were worse things than not fitting in.

Also for me, there was the ever-present, gnawing doubt that if my best judgment had failed once before, how could I trust myself again? No! Settled, stamped, sealed! Singleness wins. What I did not know was that I was about to fall passionately in love.

Unplanned Events

I met Chester in an unlikely way. I hosted a dinner party for a friend who needed to "pay off" some social obligations. Chester was one of the guests. As I flurried around the dinner table, bringing fresh platters of fish and refilling water glasses, he caught my eye. I was struck immediately by his open, straightforward manner, his clear-blue eyes and the integrity I sensed about him. There was a certain manner about him that reminded me of my father. Just as quickly, I put him out of my mind.

"Be safe and single, don't even entertain it," I told myself.

Chester's name came up a few weeks later in a conversation. I heard that he was getting out of his marriage. Knowing first hand how much pain that involved, I felt sorry for him.

Later that fall, I heard Chester speak at the University of Florida at an Energetics Seminar. I was impressed, but felt too self-conscious and shy to speak to him.

Why did I feel so attracted? Again, I tried to put him out of my mind and thought I had succeeded.

In late October, I flew to Kentucky to interview for a statewide Human Services position. What a great opportunity. For me, it would be a new beginning and certainly an end to my ongoing financial pressures. The people, the area and the job description were great.

"Why aren't you more excited?" I asked myself, flying home. Suddenly, thirty-three thousand feet above the earth, I knew. I didn't want to leave Gainesville before I had the opportunity of getting to know that clear-eyed man of integrity. Oh, drat!

A few days after I returned home, I called Kentucky and told them I wasn't interested in the job. I really felt crazy.

A month passed. A friend, Tom Robertson, and I were preparing to teach an Energetics Seminar for a group of Florida school teachers. Stuck in one area of our preparation, Tom decided to call on Chester's expertise. The three of us had a business meeting, discussing the pros and cons of various approaches. I was trying to take notes, but alas! I found myself looking at Chester and promptly forgetting everything he had just said.

"Pay attention, Betsy, this is ridiculous," I inwardly warned myself.

Afterwards, Chester asked me if I would like to come by the University to see his analog computer.

"Yes, yes, of course." I could feel the excitement.

Then shocking myself, I blurted out, "Actually, no, I don't think so. The main reason I would be doing that would be to spend time with you. I'm really not interested in computers. Thanks anyway."

The raw nerve of truth had been exposed. What had I done? I wanted to get away. Feeling very single, but not very safe, I made an excuse to exit.

The next day Chester phoned my house.

"Thank you for being honest with me yesterday," he began. "I asked you to see my computer because I wanted an excuse to spend time with you. I've been thinking a lot about you ..."

Chester sounded so straight, so genuine. It was the first time I knew that the attraction was mutual. When I got off the telephone, I looked in the mirror to see if I still looked "normal."

And so we began our relationship. Time was at a premium in both of our lives. Mostly it was phone talk after my children were in bed.

A Challenge

It didn't take long to realize that Chester and I couldn't have been more different. I loved people, he loved computers. I enjoyed crowds and activity, he preferred solitude. I wanted to walk on the good, solid earth, he wanted to swim under the sea with scuba gear or pilot a small plane high into the clouds. I adored children; this was not his strong suit. I had fairly close family ties, his were much looser.

Our backgrounds had prepared us for different things. I had grown up in a Christian home with a strong God focus. In addition, my environment was an academic community where certain types of refinements, such as English and table manners, were taken for granted as life skills. Chester had grown up on a ranch in Eastern Oregon where these kinds of things were not the priority. When there were thousands of acres of wheat to be harvested, good planning, perseverance and mechanical skills were what counted.

We came from such different geographical areas. I truly had no frame of reference to understand his western cultural background, nor he my southern one. The fact that my great-grandfather Smith was Stonewall Jackson's aide-de-camp didn't impress him at all. I knew only a little about the Oregon Trail and even less about agriculture or engineering.

Our educations were also quite different. My degrees were in Philosophy, English and Counselor Education. His were in Mechanical and Nuclear Engineering.

Chester had grown up with a totally different orientation, frame of reference and way of looking at life. Try putting all of our differences together and what do you get? A Challenge, a Big, Horrendous Challenge!

In spite of all of our differences, my once-tight grip on remaining single was rapidly loosening. This very different man was capturing my heart. This time, however, I knew that I needed more than love to make it work.

"Chester," I said solemnly, wondering how he was going to react, "I don't believe that marriage can work without the Lord being at the center of it."

He listened thoughtfully, but didn't comment. A few weeks later, we decided that we would attend a life-giving Methodist Church.

"Lord," I prayed, "what shall I do? You know that more than anything, I want to serve You. Can that still happen if I marry this engineer?"

For the first time in a long while there was a deep, abiding peace in my heart. I recognized that peace as God's answer.

Before I go on with my story, however, let me bring you up to date with Chester, the man I was to marry a year and a half later.

Chester

Historical perspective is always of value, for we do not arrive full-blown on the scene of life as a separate entity. Each of us is part of a family: a family with its own unique experiences, secrets, triumphs and tragedies; a family with its history and traditions. So please come back with me a few years, to put Chester's life into a family context.

Wilma Dyer

The year is 1873. A young boy, Jim Dyer, has just come with his family to Oregon. They had forged their way westward from Missouri, traveling in covered wagons along with several other families. At last they came to the end of the Oregon Trail. Jim's family settled in the Willamette Valley, where he grew up. As a young man, he migrated to eastern Oregon near Condon. After working for several ranchers, he started homesteading his own land. As he began to prosper, he married a petite, but sturdy woman. They raised two sons and five daughters. Wilma was their third oldest child.

Wilma was tall and strong and like the others, helped with the never-ending chores as well as with the younger children. Jim Dyer had ambitious plans for his growing family. He eventually sent five of his seven children, including Wilma, to the new land-grant college, Oregon State College in Corvallis, Oregon.

Hank Kylstra

As Jim Dyer's bustling brood was growing into maturity, one state north, in the beautiful Yakima Valley of Washington, a staunch, strongly-opinionated Dutchman, John Kylstra, had just arrived from Holland. He was accompanied by his wife, two teenage sons John and Henry (often called Hank) and two daughters, Wilma and Marie. Later, a third daughter, Peggy, was born.

As a minister in the Dutch Reformed Church, John Kylstra had experienced religious persecution and restricted opportunity. He was seeking freedom for the expression of his deep convictions and a place to experiment and grow.

Tradition also has it that while still in Holland, he had eaten one of the luscious Yakima apples and decided to come to America and grow all of the apples that he could eat!

John Kylstra, affectionately called "Pa" by many of his clan, was a man who risked much to seek his dreams. Like others of the Kylstra family, he carried within himself an independent stubbornness, characteristic even today of those Dutchmen from that section of Holland called Friesland. A man of vision, he also had hopes and visions of great opportunities for his family as they began life anew in the land of America.

Settling in "apple country," Pa was quick to develop a thriving orchard. He also pioneered in developing hybrid corn and other vegetables. He was soon selling seeds to catalogue companies. He prospered and a few years later was able to help send his sons, John and Hank, to college.

Traditionally, the men of the Kylstra family were "schooled," mostly entering into the professions of medicine, engineering, or the clergy. Pa Kylstra's two boys were born engineers.

Married

It was at Oregon State that Hank Kylstra met Wilma Dyer. After he received his degree in Mechanical Engineering and she her degree in Education, they married in 1925. The newlyweds moved to California, where Hank had gotten a job with Western Bell Telephone Company. Hank did well at his job and was soon promoted.

Over the next seven years, this happy, devoted couple had two children, Joan and Chester. In their day-by-day lives, there was nothing to hint of the tragedies that lurked just ahead, the events that would so devastate the lives of this thriving, little family.

Catastrophe

The events that led to the catastrophe happened this way. Hank's older brother John, upon finishing his education at Washington State, took a job at Boeing Aircraft in Seattle. With his dash of genius, he eventually became Chief Engineer at Boeing.

Then, in March, 1939, came the historic flight of the much-acclaimed Strataliner, the first all-metal airliner. All of the test flights of this state-of-the-art magnificent plane had been completed, the last details checking out flawlessly. The proud Boeing hosts were assembled to take the official delegates of the Netherlands Airlines for a demonstration flight. These delegates had come to negotiate the purchase of this superb airplane for their airline.

The skies were clear that Saturday afternoon. A few families waited, cheering below, as the silver-white bird rose like a falcon off of the runway. It seemed to climb effortlessly, leaving the soundless "wavers" dwarfed below.

Within fifteen minutes, those watching the plane saw an almost unbelievable sight. The plane began to turn strangely and dive toward the earth. It crashed within plain view of thirty eyewitnesses. John Kylstra, along with the flight crew and the entire Dutch delegation, passed instantly through the veil of death. The shocking news spread rapidly across the country. The Strataliner had crashed! No one was spared.

Two thousand people attended the funeral of the ten men three days later. Heavy hearted, Chester's father, Hank, left California to attend the funeral of his only brother. Hank had shared with John the precious childhood memories of dikes and wooden shoes, the adventure of crossing the ocean and the work of helping their dad make a go of the farming.

Now John was gone. He left behind a traumatized brother, grieving parents and a lovely bride of only six months. It was as if the first and the last chapters of the book had been written and the book closed, without writing the intervening chapters.

To Hank, the suddenness and the magnitude of the tragedy made what had happened seem almost unreal.

Loss

Who can fully understand another man's loss? For Hank Kylstra, the grief did not subside. It did not follow the expected pattern. Instead, as the days passed, it only seemed to intensify. Neither seven-year-old Joan, nor his two-year-old son, Chester, could break through his depression. It was as if his heart were overburdened, laden not only with the grief of his own loss, but also with the additional grief of the families from his native Holland. He personally visited each family after the crash, sharing in their trauma.

Wilma had no words to explain to her little son the depth of what his father was going through, why he didn't respond when Chester came to his knee, wanting to play. She could only tell him years later, "Your father was never the same after he returned from John's funeral."

Hank, depressed and exhausted, caught pneumonia. Less than a year after his brother's fatal crash, Hank too, was dead.

Pa and Ma Kylstra, who had risked so much for freedom and for quality of life, buried their two grown sons in the new land: Hank, thirty-nine and John, age forty-three. Wilma Dyer Kylstra, a young mother with two growing children, became a widow. Two-year-old Chester was now without a father. It was a turning point in his young life.

Growing Up

The following years are mostly a blur for Chester, as his mother struggled to go on with her life. There was a short-duration stepfather, a move to Oregon and back, and then a return to Oregon again.

Through the years, Wilma found a variety of ways to make ends meet. She was a tax attorney's secretary, ran a dress shop and eventually bought a small ranch (by eastern Oregon standards), the "Bar Z." A strong and enterprising woman, she kept herself too busy to give room to self-pity, but the fact remained that she had lost the love of her life and Chester had lost the man who had fathered and loved him.

Chester's earliest memories are of being picked on at school and of being teased by his older sister and her friends. In most situations, he felt like an "outsider." Something was missing. He didn't know what it was, but he accepted as fact that it would not change. He was just "different."

After his mother moved back to Condon, Oregon, Chester would spend weekends roaming Thirty Mile Creek, staying with his Uncle Eck and Aunt Lita on their ranch. They kept a big pot of navy beans simmering on the back stove. There was always enough for Chester to take as much as he wanted and to "make himself at home." Uncle Eck had a fondness for peacocks and kept many of these beautiful creatures as pets. They would screech and spread out their blue-green feathers and plumage, as Chester would bring out their feed.

Eck and Lita had a warm hearth and even warmer hearts for this lanky youngster, growing up with no real dad. Eck especially went out of his way to give that word of encouragement, that pat on the back, or to spend time teaching Chester the things a man in those parts needed to know. Eck and Lita were raising two boys of their own, one big and robust, the other confined to a wheel chair, but they didn't mind making room for one more.

Wilma married again, to another man who helped her work the ranch and share her life. While he was a good man and a hard worker, he had little ability to relate to the quiet, strong-willed, loner Chester had become.

Teenage years brought happier times, as Chester and his five boy-cousins tinkered on old cars and trucks together, worked the wheat and hay fields, helped in the harvest and sheep shearing and drove to the neighboring towns for the Saturday night square dances.

"Where is the square dance this weekend?" Jimmy Dyer asked, making his crew cut stand up with "bear grease."

The square dance band went from town to town. Chester and his cousins would pile into whoever's truck was running and follow the band, making new friends in the neighboring communities

Chester also liked solitude. Taking his dog Rascal, he went into the nearby mountains to hunt or hike. Sometimes, he rode his contrary Indian Pony "Lady," with whom he had an ongoing contest of wills. In dealing with Lady, his heritage as a "stubborn Dutchman" paid off.

New Vistas

School, Chester remembers, as a monotonous series of gray-colored classes, relieved only by 4-H Club projects, such as raising livestock. He and his friends would take the 4-H projects to local fairs. His motivation and his grades were both well below average. In the tenth grade, however, when all the students in Wheeler County High School were required to take a series of national achievement tests, his teachers were shocked. He not only ranked high in his school, but also on the national averages. One particular teacher, Mrs. Simpson, took a special interest in him.

"You've got to take geometry, two years of algebra and get yourself ready for college," she insisted.

Chester wasn't so sure that he wanted to do all of this.

Mrs. Simpson also encouraged Chester to enter a United Nation's essay and speech contest. She was surprised (but not as surprised as he was), when he won from his region. The reward for winning was the opportunity to travel across the United States to the UN with a group of thirty outstanding teen leaders from Oregon, Washington, British Columbia and Alberta.

Suddenly, for the first time, Chester was together with a group of young people who were going somewhere. They had ideas. They had visions of becoming somebody, of making an impact with their lives. During that summer, a dream began to come alive within Chester. By the end of the trip, his focus in life had shifted from becoming, "The best auto mechanic in eastern Oregon," to going on to college and becoming an engineer.

What a scramble to get ready for college! He was beginning his senior year of high school and had only a year to prepare. Logically, it seemed impossible. He needed two years of Algebra to apply for Oregon State. Mrs. Simpson, his mentor, only knew Algebra I. She came up with a plan.

"Chester, do you think you could figure out Algebra II if I ordered the teacher's manual for you to study along with the Algebra II book? We could arrange for you to take it by extension."

"Sure," he agreed. "I'll give it my best." The plan worked.

Actually, he finished Algebra II before Algebra I, applied to Oregon State College and was there the following fall in the freshman engineering class.

College
There was an abrupt change of scene and mood once Chester reached Corvallis.

"Look at the person on your right and on your left. One of them will be gone by the end of your freshman year. If you graduate with your engineering degree four years from now, neither one of them will be graduating with you. Only about one third of you are going to make it." These were the dean's opening words to the two-thousand new engineering freshman.

Not exactly a warm greeting, not exactly like Mrs. Simpson's encouraging words, but Chester responded with a staunch determination to be among those who graduated.

College was not easy. Chester was not prepared for a rigorous engineering curriculum. His classmates from the big city schools had not only taken their two years of algebra, but chemistry, trigonometry and beginning calculus as well. During his freshman year, he almost failed first year algebra.

"Maybe the Dean was right," he thought more than once. "Maybe next fall I will be back on the ranch finishing out the wheat harvest, one of the casualties of the freshman engineering program."

He thought about the heat and the sweat. He thought about the wheat chaff piling up on his bare skin, threatening to start itching "like crazy" if he as much as touched it.

"That's not what I want. I think I will try to make it." With even more determination to succeed, he hired a tutor.

Chester had a sinking feeling as he opened the envelope containing his first quarter's grades. What did it contain? He passed! What a relief. He was still in college. He was still among the freshmen who were making it through their first year.

Once through that difficult first quarter, he continued to catch up and to do better, feeling more at home with each passing quarter.

At night, Chester worked loading frozen foods into delivery trucks. Besides earning a minimum wage, he got to take home all of the out-of-date frozen food he wanted. Each summer, he shot a beef from the "Bar Z" herd and a venison from among the deer that grazed on the ranch. These he put into a freezer and lived on beef steak, venison and frozen foods throughout the school year. He hardly needed a food budget. This was "good living."

Chester loved music and dancing and somehow found time for both in between solving equations. Known as "The Outlaw" on a local radio station, he would play his guitar, sing and yodel. Local people would call in with requests.

"Oh, Outlaw, you sounded sooooo good! Would you play that same song next week too? That's my favorite." His fans added to the fun.

One year, Chester needed to make some money and he also wanted to meet some girls. He put his years of square dancing to good use and got a job teaching ball room dancing. It was a big success. Now he was an engineering cowboy who knew the "cha cha" and the "rumba."

It was at a folk dancing class at Oregon State where he met a lovely, tall young woman named Pat. Like Chester, she had a

Dutch heritage. They dated and courted, courted and dated, until they were sure they were meant for each other.

Chester's final two years with almost all engineering courses went much better. He was enjoying the problem solving, the "figuring out" aspect of applying God's laws that govern the universe to real-life situations.

He graduated with honors, with a Mechanical Engineering degree with an Aeronautical Engineering minor. At the same time, he was commissioned as a second lieutenant in the US Air Force. Chester was the only student from his high school class to finish a four-year college degree.

Later that summer, he married his college sweetheart, Pat.

Air Force

The Air Force moved Chester and Pat to Florida, where he became a member of the Air Force Missile Launch Team at Cape Kennedy. He was given many opportunities to learn about the various rockets the Air Force was using, such as the Snark, the Jupiter and then the Titan. He liked to joke about his responsibility as the Titan Chief Launch Officer of the Pressurization, Propellant and Propulsion Systems; "If my systems don't go, nobody's systems go."

In reality, he found that he was much more interested in creating and designing rockets than in testing them after somebody else had designed them. It furthered his determination to go to graduate school so he could get into the research and development end of things.

Chester applied to the Atomic Energy Commission for a Nuclear Engineering Fellowship for graduate studies. To his amazement, he was granted the fellowship to start school the coming fall. Great, but now, how could he get off of the Air Force rocket launch team to go back to school?

Chester wrote a letter, based on an obscure Air Force regulation, requesting an "early out" from the Air Force for "the good of the country." This was not as bad as it sounds.

His point was that the country and Air Force would benefit more if they let him accept the AEC fellowship and become a Nuclear Engineer working on nuclear rockets than if he continued to serve the remaining years of his obligation. He used his special interest in nuclear powered rockets to make his point clear.

This letter went up the chain of command all the way to the Pentagon. It then worked its way back down.

One day Chester was called into his commanding officer's office. With both enthusiasm and reluctance, he handed the letter to Chester.

"They have approved it," he said with some surprise, "at all levels. You are going back to civilian life! We're going to miss you around here but, 'good luck.'"

As Chester looks back on that time in his life and rereads the letter that he wrote, it is so clear to him that the letter was actually written by the Holy Spirit. The level of maturity, the sophisticated way the government regulations were applied and the tightness of the logic, were all way beyond his ability as a young, second lieutenant.

Graduate School

Chester and Pat moved to Gainesville, Florida, where he entered the Nuclear Engineering Department at the University of Florida in 1960. He jumped right into a wide variety of classes, all designed to equip him to handle the "secrets" of the nucleus so that mankind could benefit from this enormous source of energy.

He particularly enjoyed the numerical analysis courses and the possibility of using computers to solve tough problems. There was only one computer on campus, the first one IBM built. It was called the IBM 650. It had 2000 memory locations on a rotating drum. It used "punched" cards for both input and output. It was a nightmare by today's standards, but it drew Chester like a moth is drawn to the light. It allowed him to occupy his analytical mind with total concentration on problem solving and not on having to deal with people. Actually, it served as the perfect escape for the loner from eastern Oregon.

For his Masters' Thesis, Chester decided to develop a computer program to solve the problem of designing a nuclear rocket reactor. After all, the Air Force had let him out early "for the good of the country." Now, he needed to produce.

He spent grueling hours in the library, drawing out the equations for fluid flow, the properties of liquid and boiling hydrogen (the propellant) and of course, the nuclear reactor theories. Somehow he combined them all into a group of equations that represented the whole system. He then wrote a Fortran computer program to solve them. The Nuclear Engineering department made an investment in his work.

"We will buy you one hour of computer time on the Martin Marietta Company's IBM 740 computer in Orlando, Florida, for $500," they said to him, "so you can run the cases for your thesis."

That wasn't very much time, but he needed the most "modern, sophisticated" machine available to do his job. His whole thesis depended on the results of his complex equations and the test cases.

Chester camped out in Orlando for one week, while he worked with the IBM 740. It took 58 minutes of his precious hour of computer time just to work the "bugs" out of the program. He calculated and recalculated until he was sure that all of its various parts were working correctly. It took another 1 1/2 minutes to run the 60 cases. The job was done with thirty seconds to spare!

Once again, unbeknownst to Chester, God's hand had intervened in his life.

After the Masters Thesis, Chester proceeded on through the Nuclear Engineering program. He graduated in 1963, with a Ph.D. in Nuclear Engineering and Science.

Professional Life

Because of his nuclear rocket thesis, Chester already had contacts with people working in advanced research. He was quickly hired by TRW Systems in Redondo Beach, California. He was at last on the "creating and designing" end of the business. He got to satisfy his heart's desire to work on lots of esoteric projects, analyzing and creating computer programs to solve the difficult problems.

The time came, however, when he sensed that the national emphasis on the aerospace industry was beginning to wane. He was also feeling a yearning to go back to the university and to have a life of teaching and independent research. Little did he know that God was preparing him, putting him into just the right place where his teaching gift could be developed and sharpened and where he would be forced to learn some "people skills."

The Perfect Job

Chester returned to the University of Florida in 1967, back to the same Nuclear Engineering department where he had once been a student. For him, it was the ideal job. Now he could teach the subjects he loved, solve complex research problems using the computer and enjoy taking home a good pay check. What a life!

The only fly in the ointment was that Chester's single-focused attention on his work was having the expected negative effects on his marriage. By this time, Chester and Pat had a son Eric and a baby on the way.

"Couldn't you spend a little more time with me and the children?" Pat asked, getting tired of being a "workaholic's" widow and of trying to be the wife of a loner.

"What would we do? What is there to talk about?" Chester wondered.

Captivated by and also hiding behind the challenges of work, he continued for the next six years in his work-driven patterns.

The breach between him and Pat grew wider. What he saw was that he was becoming more and more a success at the university. What he didn't see was that he was becoming more and more a failure at home.

By 1973, he had a seven-year-old son Eric and a five-year-old daughter, Pam, who wanted their daddy. Unfortunately, their daddy hadn't had a daddy and he didn't know how to be one for them.

Enough was enough. Eventually, what had once been dissatisfaction grew into a stormy atmosphere and then into hurricane proportions. Even efforts toward reconciliation through counseling didn't help. It seemed to be too late. Divorce was chosen as the solution.

Chester and Pat, like James and I, didn't have the spiritual resources to bring God's redemptive healing into their situation. When I met Chester, he was a very broken man.

New Beginnings

The woman who had vowed to remain single fell wonderfully and passionately in love. Fortunately, most of our problems don't stop us from attraction, affection and love.

Chester and I were married in August, 1975, after a year and a half of dating. We had a simple ceremony at a Presbyterian Church in Gainesville, Florida, each of us having one special friend in attendance. My two children, James and Lewis, were with my parents in Davidson. Chester's children, Eric and Pam, were living with his former wife. I was thirty-five, Chester thirty-nine.

"Lord," I said quietly in between the "I wills." "I'm trusting You in this new beginning. I'm trusting You to help me make this work."

Clashes

When opposites attract, just like warm and cold air masses coming together, there's going to be thunder and lightning. We had lots of fireworks in our new life together along with the fresh tenderness of love and fulfillment.

There were lovely times: cheesy egg omelets eaten on a tray in bed, a boating trip to the Florida Keys, redecorating our house together and playing soccer in the yard with our children.

There were also charged times. Then the lightning would flash and the thunder roar. The main problem was that frequently, we didn't see "eye to eye." It was a tough job, trying to get our "eyes" to line up. Our everyday personality and background differences were compounded by our "unhealedness." Chester still carried a lot of rejection and "loner" tendencies from his childhood, as well as a strong undercurrent of anger.

"I like computers," he told me one day, "but not people."

In addition, he had not allowed himself the needed time to resolve and heal from the issues of his earlier marriage.

I was not a real gem myself. I had been single for so long that I was used to being the boss (not what he had in mind). Inside of myself, my dark side was as black as ever. Amidst the lightning flashes and rumblings, I was determined to work out the differences. "This marriage isn't going to fail!" I vowed.

Run the Eggs

A few weeks after our wedding, the reality of marrying an engineer hit me with its full implications. I had already learned that engineers liked to "run things," but had no clue as to what a large sphere of "things" were included. One lazy Saturday morning, I was in the kitchen beating some eggs to scramble, when Chester called from the other room.

"I'll put some dishes on the table. You run the eggs."

"Run the eggs? Run the eggs? Whoever heard of 'running' the eggs!"

To please my engineer, I got those eggs in the frying pan and "ran" them for all they were worth.

"This marriage is going to work even if I have to 'run' the waffles tomorrow!"

Children

Now, in addition to reconciling the rough edges of our own souls, we had four children who were also trying to adjust to a new family situation. James was eleven, Eric ten, Lewis nine and Pam seven. Eric and Pam, living with their mother, were often with us for weekends. For starters, six of us made a lot of bodies. It also produced a quantum leap in the possibilities of people being upset with each other at any given moment.

Chester's children were bright and attractive youngsters. We all did pretty well until it came to the spaghetti sauce. Have you ever been "done in" by the spaghetti sauce? Well, I came close.

There we were, gathered around my oval table for a happy family supper. My spaghetti sauce, one of my specialties, was hot and steaming, with the whole cloves I used in seasoning peeking out. Delicious, spicy smells filled the air, yielding a perfect atmosphere for a jovial family meal.

"I don't want any spaghetti. I want peanut butter and jelly," came from Pam and Eric's side of the table. "Do I have to eat it?"

The sad reality was that I just didn't fix my spaghetti sauce the way their mom did and the way they liked it. They were disappointed and wanted something familiar. The peanut butter and jelly jars were brought to the table. Logically, I understood. Inside, my dark side jumped at the opportunity.

"See, your spaghetti sauce isn't as good as their mom's," it taunted. "Nothing you cook is as good as her cooking!"

With a vengeance, I told it to, "Shut up!"

The children chattered on about their summer swimming classes while I tried to logically talk myself into a better emotional frame of mind.

"Betsy, remember, you are the adult here. They are children and they are doing the best they can. They didn't choose this situation. It doesn't matter whether or not they like your spaghetti sauce. Don't major on the minors."

Little mini-lectures helped to drown out my nagging inner voice.

"One day," I assured myself, "I'm going to get rid of that accusing monster."

Anybody who has tried to bring two families together knows that it takes at least the wisdom of Solomon. At times, Solomon was "nowhere" to be found. Long showers and urgent "911" prayers were my substitutes.

"God, please get me through the next few hours. Don't let me speak before I think. Lord, give me a love for my new children and if possible, vice versa. Lord, could they love each other, or is that asking too much?"

The changes I was making in my approach to eggs and in my accommodation to a family of six, however, were minor when compared to the paradigm shift that was about to take place in our spiritual lives together and in my theology. Change sometimes comes so unexpectedly.

God's Hand

Pneumonia

Fall of 1975 (mid-October to be exact), both James and Lewis got sick with pneumonia. Frazzled and exhausted from the stresses of my new life and from nursing them, I contracted it as well. Unlike them, however, I did not respond so effectively to the medication. Instead, I developed a severe allergic reaction. A rotten smell came from my lungs as I rasped and wheezed. I felt like things were crawling on my skin.

"Honey, you look green," Chester said, coming home from the University for lunch.

"Call the doctor," I insisted. "I've got to have a medication to counteract this allergic reaction."

Chester was sympathetic, but then suggested something that was a total surprise.

"Why don't we try praying first? We can call the doctor after that if needed."

Surprised, but too sick to discuss it, I lay down on my big, old-fashioned, hand-carved bed, trying not to sputter so I could hear the prayer. He wasted no words.

"God, we need your help. If You are really there, I ask You to heal my wife."

In its simplicity, Chester's prayer reminded me of one of my dad's school bus prayers; direct and to the point. As I lifted my head and began to give Chester the doctor's telephone number, I realized that my skin wasn't crawling any more. Actually, I was feeling much more peaceful and even a little sleepy.

"I believe I'll just take a nap first and then call the doctor," I murmured, snuggling down into the pillows and turning off the light. When I woke up, however, I had the shock of my life. I was ninety percent healed!

Neither Chester nor I knew that God healed people today. If someone had told us, we wouldn't have believed them. We were both amazed at what had transpired.

"It's probably just a temporary healing," I said, getting out of bed to fix supper for the first time in a week. "In all likelihood, I'll be sick tomorrow and back in bed."

Come tomorrow, however, I found the pneumonia, with its deep lung pain and its rotten stench, was permanently gone. My lungs were mostly clear.

I put fresh, sweet-smelling sheets on the bed, washed my pneumonia nightgown and prepared to go back to my job at the community college the following day. It's an understatement to say that God had gotten our attention!

More Healing
We experienced additional significant healings that first year of our marriage. One was long distance.

We had flown over to the coast for a weekend getaway. Shortly after we reached our Fernandina Beach destination, our baby-sitter, Virginia, had called to tell us that Lewis had a fever of 103 degrees. Unable to fly back because of a tornado watch, we were stuck.

I was upset, really upset. I was ready to start walking home. My baby was sick and needed me. It wasn't the same for him to be sick with a baby-sitter. I paced the floor wringing my hands for a while and then, helpless and frustrated, sat down in the middle of the floor. Silent tears were trickling down my cheeks.

Chester gently sat down beside me. "Remember last November when God healed you of pneumonia?" he asked.

At first, I didn't get the connection.

"Let's try prayer. Maybe it will work again. We've got nothing to lose." (Engineers are very pragmatic.)

We bowed our heads. "Lord, our little boy is so sick and we can't get home. Please heal whatever is causing his high fever." Opening our eyes, we looked at each other, wondering if God would answer our prayer.

Twenty minutes later, the motel phone rang.

"I don't know what has happened," Virginia said, "but Lewis is up and running around. He wants to go outdoors and play. Shall I let him? He seems fine now. His temperature is normal!"

We knew exactly what had happened.

"Thank You, Lord, for healing our son," we said, overcome with awe. I couldn't ever remember feeling more grateful.

It's a funny thing about God's healing. Once you have experienced it personally, no one can talk you out of it. It is settled.

These experiences of physical healing brought us light-years closer to God as our loving Father.

"God, You really do see and care about what is happening in our everyday lives."

I remembered the story of Jesus healing the centurion's servant long distance.[1] That was pretty miraculous, but not nearly as special as His healing our Lewis.

We had experienced a miracle and we wanted to get closer to this God who heals little boys long distance. We didn't know what to do next, but we were convinced of this: when very ordinary people pray, extraordinary things can happen.

---

[1] Luke 7:1-10

A Different Kind of Healing

There is no question in my mind that our God provides great comfort. I have experienced it numerous times through prayer and scripture. God has brought His comfort in times of death, sickness, crises and lack. He has brought it in times of great uncertainty. I counted on His comfort as a gift, there for me when I needed it. I had always assumed that when Jesus talked about healing the broken hearted,[1] He was referring to the kind of healing comfort with which I was familiar.

Max Lucado, in his book, *He Still Moves Stones*,[2] asks some interesting questions about emotional healing.

> Why did God leave us one tale after another of wounded lives being restored? So we could be grateful for the past? So we could look back with amazement at what Jesus did?
>
> No. No. No. A thousand times, No. The purpose of these stories is not to tell us what Jesus did. Their purpose is to tell us what Jesus does.
>
> "Everything that was written in the past was written to teach us," Paul penned. "The Scripture gives us patience and encouragement so that we can have hope."[3]
>
> These are not just Sunday school stories. Not romantic fables. Not somewhere-over-the-rainbow illusions. They are historic moments in which a real God met real pain so we could answer the question, "Where is God when I hurt?"
>
> He's not doing it just for them. He is doing it for me. He's doing it for you.

[1] Luke 4:18

[2] Lucado, Max, *He Still Moves Stones*, Word Publishing, Dallas, TX, 1993, page 200.

[3] Romans 15:4

Max Lucado is talking about more than comfort. He is talking about more than Jesus healing in the past. He is talking about Jesus intervening and healing our real pain today. He is implying that Jesus can touch the pain of our dark side, of our great disappointments and of our tragedies. Today!

In 1977, we were in a different world than Max Lucado. We were not thinking the same kinds of thoughts or raising the same questions. Long before Chester or I read about Jesus healing the inner person, or had any revelation of it through the scriptures, we experienced it.

God was about to touch us in ways that would change our lives. We were in for more of His surprises!

Chester's Experience

Because of the emotional abandonment he had experienced as a child, Chester had never felt that he "belonged." This feeling made it hard for him to put down roots or to relate to people. But one day ...

It was a hot, summer day and we were driving Old Blue, our re-modeled van, over to Crescent Beach, Florida. Actually, I was driving and Chester was on the bed in the back, relaxing and praying. All of a sudden, I heard deep sobs coming from him, a crescendo of gut-rending sounds. I had never heard him cry at all, much less pour out such unleashed emotion. Both curious and alarmed, I forced myself to quietly wait until the paroxysm ceased. I hoped he would want to share.

For a long time, he was unable to talk. Then he moved to the front of the van, smiling and radiant. Now I was really puzzled.

"I don't really have words to describe what happened," he said, the amazement clear in his hushed voice. "All I can tell you is that the very God of the universe wants a Father-son relationship with me! I have been experiencing the awesomeness of His love."

The tears came again. Through words and images, God had revealed Himself to Chester as the Father he had never had, as a personal Father-God who loved and cherished him and who wanted a close relationship with him.

Years ago, a shell had formed around his heart. Imperceptibly, this shell had started forming when he lost his dad. Then, it had grown thicker and more rigid as he was rejected by two stepfathers and experienced rejection by school-mates. An impermeable barrier, this shell had effectively locked him in and others out. It was locking up his ability to give or receive love in an intimate, wholehearted way.

Now this invisible, destructive shell was beginning to disintegrate, melting under the heat and irresistible tenderness of God's love for him as a special son. It was the most important thing that he needed in his life.

Over the next months, I watched as Chester began to move out of his "loner" patterns, as he stopped hiding himself away. He was like a newly transplanted plant, who at last had put his roots down in the fertile soil of God's love. He began to grow. It was only a few short years before he would proudly announce one day, "You know, I'm beginning to like people almost as much as I like computers!" (Miracles still happen.)

My Experience

My first experience of God touching me in a similar way occurred about two years later, one winter Sunday night.

Jackie Canapa, a faith-filled friend, was visiting that evening. The children had said their "Good Nights," and we were talking and sipping peppermint tea.

"Betsy," she said, as the evening progressed, "I believe that we should pray. I have a real sense that there is something Jesus wants to touch in your life."

Neither of us knew what it might be. A few moments later, Jackie continued.

"Just bow your head and ask Jesus to come and heal you."

I had never done anything like this before and was a little nervous, yet I trusted Jackie.

As I followed her suggestion, I began to see a picture of a tiny baby girl who had just been born. This baby was a deep, rosy pink and was waving her little arms in the air.

It was a lot like watching a movie. I was an observer, watching scene by scene as the story unfolded.

All of a sudden, I knew that the baby girl I was seeing was me! Filled with amazement, I watched as a man came into the room. I recognized immediately that the man was Jesus. He picked me up, looking at me with great delight. The tender expression on His face, the beam in His eyes, was like that of a proud papa who is absolutely thrilled.

"I'm so glad that you are here," He said, adoringly. "I planned for your life a long time ago." He paused. "I won't tell you yet about everything that I have for you to do, but you are going to love it. I have chosen you and I have chosen you to do something special for Me. You are going to be so fulfilled."

Then He patted me, snuggling me against His shoulder. He was loving me so tenderly, as if I were the only baby in the world.

The scene began to fade. I came back to the present, to my living room, to Jackie and to Chester.

The torrent of weeping that followed was an upheaval of the deep; those deeply hurting places in my life where, ever since high school, the wretched lies had lived. These lies had convinced me that, "I was a mistake," that, "I was only a trespasser in life," and that, "I had no right to exist!"

What I had seen was real and I knew that it was real. I knew that I hadn't made it up. It was as real as the physical healing I had experienced from pneumonia.

The Lord's words to me struck a powerful blow to the lies I had believed. He had **planned** me. He intended for my life to have purpose and meaning. He **gave** me my right to exist. **My life** was a gift from Him. I heard these words out of His own mouth. Just as finding the precise thread is the key to unraveling the hem of a dress, so God's revelation to me put into my hand the thread to unraveling those old lies.

"I was **not** a mistake. I was **not** a trespasser on this earth. I was **not** someone who was 'never supposed to be.' I belonged! I

was planned and chosen. He intended for my life to have purpose and meaning."

These were life-changing moments. God's light had begun to penetrate my dark side.

Slowly, my life began to change. On occasions when the old, entrenched thoughts about not "having a right to exist" would come back, I had the new-found ammunition of God's revelation to resist them.

"No," I said firmly, "I'm not buying those lies anymore. No, I don't have to apologize for being here. No, I don't have to prove my worth. No, I'm not an 'inside-outsider.' I'm an 'inside-insider'!"

Now my dark side had a big hole in it. It was still there, but for the first time, I had confidence that one day I would be healed and totally free of it.

Chester, as astonished as I was, was there along with Jackie while my healing was taking place. As with our first physical healing, we thought that what had occurred was a one-time event.

"I don't understand why God is so good to me," the new "me" said as Chester and I were getting ready for bed that night. In a special way, I could join in with the Psalmist David when he said, "I will bless the Lord who has counseled me."[1]

Little did either of us know that God's direct revelation of Himself to our spirits is one of the wonderful ways that He heals His children's broken hearts.

---

[1] Psalms 16:7a NAS

Pioneering

In 1978, there was a deep stirring within both Chester and me, a restlessness, a hunger for something more. That restlessness had the same feeling as searching the refrigerator for some food that would satisfy, but not finding it. God was moving in our spirits, wooing us, calling us, but we didn't recognize Him. We did not understand that God was the author of our "divine" discontent.

Trying to understand our dissatisfaction, we reassured each other, "It's just the 'same ol', same ol' at the University and at the community college as well. Besides, our young teenage children are being offered drugs at school. We have a right to be upset, to want a change."

But somehow our explanations didn't quite fit. There was no food in the refrigerator that satisfied.

"Chester," I mused, later that year, "I have this uncanny feeling that God is trying to tell us something with this 'discontent.'"

We were learning to pray and listen to His voice through thoughts and images that came to us in prayer.

"Let's concentrate on listening for the next several weeks to see what God is say about this."

We agreed and wrote down scriptures, thoughts and impressions that came to us during our prayer times. At the end of that period, we compared notes. We each agreed that God was telling us to move!

Land Looking

In 1978, Chester took a year's leave of absence from the University of Florida and I resigned my job as Director of a Paraprofessional Counselor Training Program at Santa Fe Community College. We had never done such a radical thing before. We were trying to follow the Lord's leading!

Hoping that we weren't as weird and crazy as some of our friends thought we were, we stationed ourselves in Montreat, North Carolina, for the summer, sensing that our new home was to be in my beloved mountains.

For countless days, we trampled over mountainous terrain with enthusiastic Realtors, but we came home with only blisters and chiggers.

"Lord, did we miss You?" we wondered in our discouragement.

The Land

Then that fall we found our land, one hundred ten acres on top of a mountain near Burnsville. We were exuberant. "Breathtaking" is the best description for our new property: unspoiled, pure beauty. The land had many varieties of fruit trees, a meadow, huge rocky caves, a canyon and several streams including a beautiful waterfall. Looking from our property down into the valley, we saw the beautiful Cane River, meandering along, full of fish and inviting swimming holes. Across the valley, we could see Celo Knob and in the distance, Mt. Mitchell. When the fog would rise up out of our valley below, it looked like creation all over again. Our children called it "awesome," and they were right.

We thought we knew what we were doing. What we didn't know was that we were about to enter a five-year period of "pioneering," of going through God's wilderness,[1] during which time God would break us loose from many of our former molds and mindsets.

There is a scriptural principle describing one of God's ways: first the natural, then the spiritual.[2] He lets His people experience something in the natural, by having them walk through a life situation. Then later, there is the parallel in their spiritual lives. The natural is a type and foreshadowing of the spiritual. The physical freedom that the Israelites experienced through the Exodus, for example, was a type and foreshadowing of the spiritual freedom that God would later bring to His people through the life, death and resurrection of Jesus.

---

[1] Luke 4:1-13
[2] 1 Corinthians 15:48

81

The physical pioneering that we were entering into was one of God's ways of preparing us to be pioneers much later in the spiritual realm. We had to be willing to be trail blazers, to move out beyond our comfort zone and to trust Him.

For a woman whose dark side was just beginning to be healed, this was an immensely large step! As we drove away from Gainesville, Florida, with all of our belongings loaded in a U-Haul truck, I knew that I was leaving my comfort zone behind. Our house had been sold and there was no turning back.

"Whatever it is I am doing, Lord, let it bring me closer to You."

Mountain Life

The pioneering began with our mountain road. We approached our idyllic property from a not-very-idyllic road. Yes, we flatteringly called it a road. It was one-half mile of mud, mixed with rock; actually more like a glorified creek bed. There were days that this road was my enemy. There were days that it seemed to call out, "Just see if you can get up the mountain!" Having deep ditches on either side and muddy ruts in its middle, it ascended steeply up the mountainside to our two cabins, soon to be our new home.

They too, were far from elegant. No chandeliers! One cabin, about six hundred square feet, was livable. It was insulated, had wood paneling, a Franklin wood stove, inside plumbing and electricity. The other one, an old log cabin, lacked all such amenities. Abandoned for many years, it had become a shelter for unknown varieties of wild animals. I thrilled at the idea of reclaiming it.

We moved in January, 1979. As we built our first fire in the wood stove (our only heat), I wondered, "What will our lives be like?" There were no neighbors to borrow a lemon from and we had our own house key. So radically different for this small town, neighborhood-loving girl. We had a new geography, a new culture, a new lifestyle.

No Lack of Adventure

Two days after we arrived, it snowed. It snowed for two solid weeks. The snow covered over the grass, weighted down the bushes until their branches curled over unnaturally and touched the ground and stood up like a tall white hat on our tin roof. Foot-long icicles hung from the wooden porch railings. It was so cold that we even had ice on the inside of our bedroom windows. Finding some enticing, steep places on the property, we piled on our sleds and whizzed downhill, screaming with both fright and delight.

Lips turning blue with cold, we eventually went back inside, where I cooked scrambled eggs, crusty batter bread and made hot mugs of cocoa. Later, I put together the fixings for soup, which simmered along in a big, black kettle on top of the wood stove. It was a good beginning.

During the snows, we tried several times to rev up our van and make runs up the hill, but alas, it would slide back, coming dangerously close to the ditches on either side of our "road." So, parked it stayed, at the bottom of our hill for several weeks while we "toted" our groceries on our sleds and in backpacks. This method sufficed for our clothes as well, which had to be washed in town. (Our washing machine on the back porch was only a warm weather friend.) We hung our clothes to dry in the old tobacco barn a few hundred feet from the cabin. With the hill to navigate, wood to be brought in, the purity of our drinking water to be checked and a six mile trek into town for groceries, there wasn't too much time to get homesick.

"How are you doing in all of that snow, pioneering up there on top of the mountain?" My parents' cheerful voices were a welcome sound in the strangeness that was still ours. "We just called to check on you. Are the boys okay?"

"Yes, but this is quite an adventure," I said.

"What did you fix for supper?" Mother wanted to know, as she always did. "Do you need my recipe for vegetable soup? It would taste good in that cold weather."

Roots
Daddy was on the line too. "Did you know that my great uncle, Dr. Michael Schenck, was a circuit-riding judge and used to come to Burnsville and hold court?"

"No, Daddy, I don't ever remember your telling me that."

"Do go up to Wilson's store, further on up the Cane River. That's the area where Big Tom Wilson grew up. Remember, he's the one who discovered Elisha Mitchell's body."[1]

I had hiked around Mount Mitchell with my dad numerous times and knew the story well.

As Daddy rattled on, recounting family and local history, a transformation was taking place. Our home and our mountain top, which only a few minutes earlier had seemed so terribly re- mote, so disconnected from everything, suddenly began to be- come familiar, "connected." Just think, somebody in our very own family a generation before,had been right where we are now. By the time my parents finished talking, I felt somehow related to our land and that this was our country.

Adjustments

Some adjustments came slowly. Our move was hardest for our son's Lewis and James, who were in the seventh and ninth grades respectively. Teenagers are cliquish anyway and making new friends in a very different culture was difficult during this stage of their lives. After all, they were not the ones who had felt discontent in Gainesville. Eventually they did make friends and entered into various school activities, but they never felt that comfortable, one-hund- red-percent sense of belonging. For them, our pioneering adventure had some definite sacrifices.

Spring

Spring came. Daffodils and wild asparagus came up near our back door. Blue and purple violets erupted, blanketing the meadow. The six old apple trees that lined our driveway blos- somed out in delicate pink, reminding me of full-skirted young girls, dressed for a spring prom. Our land came alive. It was garden time. Muscles tensed as we pulled and hacked at the

---

[1] Mt. Mitchell is named after Elisha Mitchell because of his early exploring work there. Unfortunately, he died in a fall on Mt. Mitchell. Big Tom Wilson found him.

stubborn blackberry bushes that occupied the space of our garden-to-be.

"Here, a whole row is clean now."

"Bring me the soybean seeds."

"Read the directions one more time."

"When did the book say we could expect our last frost?   Are you sure we're not planting too early?"

We were going to raise and preserve our own food supply, at least as much as we were able. I had never planted anything besides zinnias. I loved watching our "dinner" come up and the fresh sweetness of the vegetables as we picked them right before supper. For the first time, I was getting ready to learn to "can" our green beans and tomatoes.

Mountain Air

Even Chester's commercial Air Taxi business "Mountain Air" had an aspect of pioneering to it. The "airport" consisted of a grass strip in a mountainous box canyon. If Chester needed to return from a flight after dark, he would circle our cabin in his small plane. That was my signal to make a dash for the airport and shine the van's headlights down the runway so he could locate the beginning of the runway. He would swoop down over the van just before the plane's tires connected with the grass. Loving life as much as I do, I evacuated the van (just in case!) and watched the landing from the sidelines.

Team

For the first time, Chester and I felt like a team. We needed each other for so many of the things that made up everyday life. We needed each other to do our dream. We needed each other to try to sense God's direction. It was very different from the days when he went his way to the University and I went mine to the Community College. We were experiencing a new interdependence, a new oneness. That too, was part of God's plan.

Unusual Friends

Our pioneering continued. The first year in the mountains we tackled the garden; the second, we took on the one-hundred-year-old log cabin. With its broken windows, pink painted door and residues of wild animals, this cabin was a good candidate for lots of TLC. There was a purpose in our refurbishing. We felt James and Lewis would each benefit from having his own bedroom and our plan was to make the second cabin useable as our bedroom. It was conveniently close by, but needed a thorough overhaul. The cabin became a family project.

"James, put on those white-mule gloves, before you pick up the insulation."

"Lewis, do you need some more paint remover for the door?"

"Mom, I think it has at least seven coats of paint on it," Lewis said, his patience wearing thin. "Anybody else want to rub on it for a while?"

"When we finish the new tin roof, we'll work on installing the picture window. We're going to need some help."

Conversation about work items drifted easily back and forth as the cabin, with its beautiful two-foot-wide logs, became transformed. Chester brought in electricity and installed a wood stove. It was becoming a jewel of a home.

One day, our son Eric let out a startled cry. Behind the board which he had just removed was a large blacksnake coiled in its nest. Both son and snake were equally surprised. This seven-and-one-half-foot creature also had a six-foot-long mate nearby. They obviously considered this cabin to be their home and were not too happy about the newcomers. Since blacksnakes are known to kill rats, mice and poisonous snakes, we decided on a policy of peaceful coexistence.

Gradually, we grew to be friends. The blacksnakes became tamer and would hang out on the rafters and watch our building project. They greatly appreciated the insulation we installed next to the tin roof. It gave them a good place to spend the day.

At night, we could hear them crawling out between the insulation and the tin roof to go hunting. They would "stair-step" down on the logs where two parts of the building made an "inside" corner on the outside of the log cabin. I never imagined that I would be able to share my bedroom with two large snakes.

Later that summer, Ed and Priscilla, some Gainesville friends, came for a weekend's visit. Sacrificially, we planned to let them stay in our lovely log cabin. As they entered the cabin and sat down on the couch, they immediately noticed a seven-foot-long snake skin, freshly shed on the back of the couch. Graciously, they declined our hospitality and opted to stay at the NuWray Inn in Burnsville. It was a little too much pioneering for their taste.

God Won't Stay in My Box

The external trappings of our pioneering lives were more evident and easier to define than the internal. Inside, our hunger for God grew. Things began to happen that were "firsts" in our lives, things that didn't fit with my theology. God wouldn't stay in my box.

Every Sunday, we met with ten other adults in the basement of the local Methodist church. We were studying the book of Acts. Somehow, both Chester and I had a deep inner knowing that the things that we were reading about in Acts were not just for the early church, but were also for us today. It didn't make sense that God would just cut off the powerful manifestations of His Spirit, the evidence that His kingdom is real.

One Sunday, Betty Mottsinger, a vibrant, older woman in our class, prayed with me to have the fullness of God's Spirit, an experience called the Baptism of the Holy Spirit. This experience further fueled my hunger pangs for a closer relationship with God, for more of Him. It also intensified my desire to read God's Word. The Bible began to yield more revelation.

"I guess that has been there all along, Lord," I said almost continuously, "but I never saw it before."

A Dream
Chester began to have some special dreams. In one dream he was walking along a road outside of a city wall. Just as he was awakening, he heard a shout, "Second Timothy one fourteen." At this point, he had learned that "Timothy" was a book in the Bible, but he had no idea what was in Timothy. He looked it up, finding,

> Guard, through the Holy Spirit who dwells in us, the treasure which has been entrusted to you.[1]

This was puzzling to say the least.

---

[1] 2 Timothy 1:14 NAS

"What treasure? Who was dwelling in him? Lord, what are You trying to say to us?"

Confusion

One evening we were attending a Full Gospel Businessmen's meeting in Asheville, North Carolina. As Chester was being prayed for by several of the men, he began to speak words in a new, unknown language. The men begin to rejoice, but Chester stopped the process.

"No, this isn't what I want. This is the same thing that I used to do as a boy in eastern Oregon while I was milking the cows. I would sing and make up this language. That's what I am doing now. I don't want this. I want the 'real' Holy Spirit."

The men insisted that what was happening was real, that the Holy Spirit was giving him the words to say, but nevertheless, he left that meeting feeling very confused.

As he prayed over the next few weeks, the Holy Spirit brought to Chester's awareness that he actually had received Jesus as an eight-year-old boy the one year he had attended a Sunday School class. There had been no follow up, but his salvation had taken place. At some point, he had received the fullness of God's Spirit. He would unselfconsciously sing and "make up" words, as twice daily he milked the cows.

He was comforted to read in a book *The Gifts of the Holy Spirit*, by Dennis and Rita Bennett, that very occasionally, children would have an early, spontaneous "filling." It became clear that God's Spirit had actually been living in Chester since childhood!

That's what "Timothy" was all about!

This revelation helped explain many things to him: God's hand of protection in times of danger, making the correct decision at critical turning points in his life, his creativity in problem solving and even our miraculous healings.

Chester and I were both very tentative about using this new prayer language. He used his only in the shower. I always closed the bedroom door before engaging in mine.

Growing up, I had made fun of such things. Only gradually did we come to understand its potential and its power.

We continued having experiences that were new for us. We did not know what to do with them, or how to think about them. We didn't have any categories of experience into which they fit.

A Song

Once when I was driving to Davidson, I heard a song being sung to me. I looked around but there was no one in sight. The words and beautiful music were filling my car. I drove over to the side of the road, grabbed a grocery receipt (which was all I could find to write on) and scribbled the words down as fast as possible, all six verses. As soon as I got to Davidson, I sang and recorded the song, so this precious gift wouldn't be lost. Here is the first verse.

> You are My Body, I have no other.
> I've told you what to do, throughout My Word.
> I've given you My Spirit,
> I've given you My Power,
> Now you must go for Me, go and do My work.

"God, You must be calling me. What is it You want me to do, what 'work?'"

After receiving my song, I had a rebuttal, additional ammunition against what was left of my dark side.

When it would say, "God will never use you for anything. You're too unworthy," I would fight back instead of being passive. I would sing my song long and loud, all six verses if I needed to.

"God **is** calling me. I just don't know to what work yet, or where He wants me to go." I picked out the tune on my banjo and sang my "call song," helping His call get more and more settled in my heart.

New experiences were happening to us. It was like a long, gentle soaking rain seeping into the ready earth, bringing forth life.

My theology was "bumfuzzled." I could see however, that what was happening to us was the operation of God's Spirit.

A Word of Knowledge

One summer day in 1981, Chester was praying for a man who had a breathing problem. All of a sudden, he had an accurate "knowing" about this man's unforgiveness towards his father. Chester was right. As the man chose to forgive and release years of bitterness, he was immediately healed of a debilitating asthmatic condition. This was the first word of knowledge that either of us had received.

We were intrigued. "God, how does one get a word of knowledge? How did Chester just suddenly come to know that information?"

That night, we looked in First Corinthians chapter twelve, a chapter describing spiritual gifts.

> Now there are varieties of gifts, but the same Spirit. And there are varieties of ministries and the same Lord. And there are varieties of effects, but the same God who works all things in all persons. But to each one is given the manifestation of the Spirit for the common good. For to one is given the word of wisdom through the Spirit and to another the word of knowledge according to the same Spirit.[1]

Our answer was right there. The Holy Spirit had brought the word of knowledge for the "good" of this man to whom we were ministering.

New experiences continued to be the norm. During 1982, I was working as the Social Worker on a Hospice team. I prayed for a terminally sick woman who had a painful cancerous tumor. It caused her whole side to protrue. As I prayed, her pain stopped. When she went to the bathroom the next morning, she eliminated a huge, gray mas. That part of her cancer was gone! I was thrilled, but the Hospice team was not.

---

[1] 1 Corinthians 12:4-8

"We are supposed to be helping these people die," one of them said angrily, "not getting them healed!"

Our Hospice patient died about a year later, but went many months without her former, agonizing pain. I was touched by God's kindness. This was one of the first prayer healings that we had seen outside of our own family.

God's Graduate Course

Our biggest theological disruption came in the fall of 1982. It had to do with the reality of demons. In this area, God got totally and completely out of my box.

You need to understand that as a Mental Health worker, I believed that "demons" were simply Biblical terminology for mental health problems, not real entities. After all, we are living in the twentieth century and have more sophisticated understandings of such things. My eyes were about to be opened.

It happened this way. Chester and I had heard of a woman named Pat Brooks who lived in Asheville. She and her husband had a "deliverance" ministry, which means that they identified and cast out demons.

When Chester suggested that maybe we should "check it out," I was not thrilled at the prospect, but I knew that **he** had an unrelenting problem with anger and that maybe **he** would get some help. Nothing else seemed to have worked and this problem was hard on all of us. Little did I know that he was going primarily because he thought **I** needed the help. We made an appointment with Pat and her husband for the following Sunday night, agreeing to read a book she had written before we came.

Meanwhile, life was happening on other fronts. Our son James had just had all of his wisdom teeth removed (under anesthesia) and was experiencing what we thought was temporary amnesia.

"At school today, I just couldn't seem to remember what my next class was," he told us.

On Friday afternoon, while I was counseling at the local Mental Health Clinic, I got a call from Dr. Carolyn Cort, our good friend and pediatrician. She told me that James had been brought to her office from school because he had been very disoriented. He couldn't find his classroom or remember his friends' names.

"I want him to be seen by a neurologist in Asheville immediately," she told me.

I canceled the rest of my appointments, called Chester to meet us in Asheville and picked up James.

A strange thing happened right after her call. I started crying and I couldn't stop. The sobs would just continue. It was as if the crying had hold of me and I had no choice.

In Ashevillle, the neurologist said that it wasn't obvious what was troubling James, that he needed more time to make a diagnosis, and to bring James back the following week.

Greatly humiliated by being out of control, I continued to cry. I was very concerned about James and his unexplained amnesia, but this incessant crying was out of proportion, crazy.

The next day, I cried in various stores as I ran my errands. I couldn't make my tears stop.

"Well, one thing for sure, I don't want to go see Pat Brooks this weekend. We have more than enough going on with James' problem and I'm so embarrassed about all of my tears." I was very insistent as I spoke to Chester.

Just then, the phone rang. It was Pat. I had been trying to get Chester to call and cancel our appointment. I certainly didn't want to speak to her. Chester began to explain about James and about my tears.

"Put Betsy on the line!" Pat demanded.

Caught in the middle, Chester was happy to hand me the phone.

I was sniffing and sobbing. Pat skipped the formalities and launched right in.

"Spirit of grief," she said, "I command you to come out of her, in Jesus' name!"

As if a faucet had been turned off, my tears stopped, dried up and vanished. I was overcome. "What did she do?" I wondered.

"Well, that takes care of the spirit of grief," Pat said. "We'll take care of the rest tomorrow night."

I decided maybe **Chester** really did need that deliverance, even more than I had thought!

Later that same evening, James got extremely sick. He began to "throw up" every fifteen minutes or so. For many hours he vomited. As he got weaker, I was helping him from his room to the bathroom and back.

It was winter and Chester and I were sleeping on the fold-out couch to be near the wood stove. Every fifteen minutes, as James and I passed by the couch, we woke Chester up again. About two AM, I said,

"Chester! I think we need to take James into the local hospital. I'm afraid that he is getting too dehydrated."

"Let me see what I can do. If I can't get whatever this is to stop, we'll take him in," Chester replied.

More than ready for his help, I laid down.

Chester did not know anything about the demonic. Where he grew up in eastern Oregon, no one had mentioned demons. Neither were they a part of our dinner time conversation.

He did know that Jesus had commanded unclean spirits out of people and that they had left.

He was angry. He knew that somehow his household was being stolen from. Something serious was troubling James; first the amnesia and now this sickness. Furthermore, he had been kept up all night. He suspected that our upcoming visit to the Brooks for our first deliverance and James' problems were connected. Demons had something to do with this whole situation.

He got ready to command out whatever was affecting James.

The Holy Spirit stopped him.

"What are you doing?" he heard in his spirit.

Chester explained that he was going to cast out whatever was bothering James.

"You don't have sufficient authority in this situation."

He was puzzled. Then, he knew. For the next ten minutes, he began to repent of being such a poor stepfather to James. In his heart that night, he received James as his own son.

Then he went back to addressing the demons.

"Whatever is in there that is stealing my son's memory, whatever is in there is making him sick, I command you demons, in the name of Jesus, to come out!"

Gradually, the trembling and the arcing of his body subsided. He begin to look less "green," and to stop shaking. He became quiet and then he drifted off to sleep!

The next morning, he felt weak, but his memory had fully returned.

When Dr. Cort examined James the following week, she said that he looked perfectly normal. She then told us that on the previous Friday, when she had first examined him, she had seen indicators of a brain tumor in the back of his eyes, on his retina. "I've never before seen it reverse!" she added.

We were thrilled, excited and delighted with God's healing of James. We never did go back to the neurologist!

Sunday night came and we kept our appointment with Pat Brooks and her husband. Unlike what I had imagined, she and her husband were nice, normal people; just zealous to see others set free.

We shared our trouble spots. For Chester, they were anger and lust. For me, they were fear and unworthiness, the main manifestations of my dark side. The Brooks took us through repentance and forgiveness and called out the appropriate demons. It was almost disappointingly tame; a few yawns and burps here and there. I wasn't sure anything was happening.

On our way out the door, Pat exclaimed, "Oh, the Lord is showing me that the two of you are going to have a ministry similar to ours!"

"Chester," I said adamantly, once we were safely back in the car, "She just lost all her credibility with me. I'm not going to have anything to do with demons!"

The next week was a good one. Our son was well again. Chester's lust was gone and his anger much abated. For me, the biggest thing I experienced was a drastic reduction of negative thoughts, especially thoughts of unworthiness and self-accusation. I had always believed that I was the source of these negative thoughts from my dark side, but now I was beginning to wonder.

Struggling with my old theology, which made no place for demons, I had to admit that they must be real. I didn't understand much about the demonic, but I did understand that my crying had suddenly stopped, that James' memory had returned and his sickness stopped. Also, after my deliverance session, most of my negative thoughts were gone. Think of it, all these years, it was demons that had been speaking these "things" to me!

Through the deliverance, my fears were greatly reduced. Lots of fears were gone, such as fear of failure and fear of rejection. But I sensed that my life-long enemy, the fear of being killed, was somehow still there. I couldn't be sure because it hadn't yet been tested.

"One of these days, I'll get totally rid of you too," I told it.

We had just gone through God's graduate-level course in demonology. My dark side was getting less and less dark.

Decision Time

People began to ask us if we were in the ministry. Maybe in a sense we were. I prayed for many of my counselees where I worked at the Community Mental Health Center and on occasion did deliverance. I saw a twelve-year-old girl suffering from anorexia totally healed and set free. Our hearts yearned to help people full-time, but we had four college-age children and had just recovered from being in debt.[1] Furthermore, we were still dealing with "worthiness" issues. We did, however, take one really big step. We sold our beloved mountaintop property and moved into a rented house, "just in case" God might call us. We wanted to be ready.

Dreams

Early in 1984, God gave Chester a series of dreams that we did not fully understand, but we felt that they related to the future direction of our lives.

In the first one, we were in basic training in the army. We were issued khaki uniforms and proceeded to have to "jump" through all of the "hoops" associated with basic training. We marched, "left turn," made beds, and responded quickly at each barked command.

About a week later, in another dream, Chester saw us being removed from basic training. We were issued new uniforms and put into special forces training, something like the Green Berets. There was lots of individual sniper activity as we hid behind trees and fired on the enemy.

Then a week later, Chester had a third dream. He saw the two of us watching a group of dark figures attacking some people playing on a baseball field. We rushed them and did hand-to-hand combat, defeating them one by one. They finally scattered in fear, happy to get away from us. We pondered what these dreams might be saying to us about our future.

---

[1] Please see our financial testimony in Part 2 of this book.

Direction

One Saturday night at our friend Betty Mottsinger's prayer meeting, a sweet-spirited elderly man, Charles Browning, was there. He was known as a man who could hear the voice of the Lord. He laid hands on us and prayed and prophesied.

> ... The Lord says that there are groups of people around the world waiting for you to bring your message. The Lord says don't wait any longer. It is time to go and be prepared.

The tears came. I could hardly believe what God was speaking through this man who had never met us, who had no knowledge of the deep desire to serve God that was harbored in our hearts.

Ever so gently God was speaking to us, "Come and be My Pioneers."

Chester was 47 and I was 44. Our first son was in college and our other three children were lined up behind him.

After some serious prayer, we made a decision. With unsteady hand, I wrote my parents and told them that we were going to quit our jobs and go to Bible College. They called back. They loved me too much to want failure for my life.

"You'll be so old when you finish. Who will want you?" they asked.

"I don't know," I said miserably, "I just know **we have to go**."

And then out loud I pleaded, "Please God, tell me just one more time this is really You."

Bible College
Making the Man (and Woman)
Before the Ministry

As we unloaded our U-Haul in Pensacola, Florida, on one of those sweltering dog days in June, 1984, I felt so confident, so trusting. "All is well with my soul," I sang, carrying in boxes and furniture, looking forward to our new life as Bible College students. We were preparing for the ministry!

Two weeks later, when the children were bored and disgruntled, when both of our air conditioners had broken and quit working and when Chester was hiding out in the back room working on the project God had provided,[1] my previously "well soul" felt like it had gangrene.

"Lord, You did call us here, didn't You?"

"You missed it," came the haunting words from my dark side, still an opportunist. "Your parents were right all along."

"No," I fought back, "God called us and we're staying."

"God," I said, "I need some kind of 'sign' that we're on the right track, that somebody knows or even cares that we're here."

Early the next morning, our phone rang. It was Burl Bagwell, a much-loved Liberty Bible College teacher. We had just met him the previous week.

"I need to go out of town next weekend and was wondering if Chester could teach my Sunday school class for me," he said. "Never before have I asked someone that I don't know well, but I felt like the Lord was prompting me to ask Chester."

As my husband came to the phone, my eyes filled with tears.

"Lord, why is it so hard for me to trust that we heard You, that we're on the right track?"

---

[1] Please see our financial testimony in Part 2 of this book.

God's Dealings

Bishop Bill Hamon, founder of Christian International Ministries, is fond of saying,

"God has to make the man before He can make the ministry."

God was about to deal with every facet of our lives, to give us a complete overhaul. We thought we were coming to Liberty Bible College for two years of "book learning." If anyone had told us in advance that His process was going to take six years, I probably would have jumped ship. (God has some well kept secrets.) We had no idea how much work God needed to do in our lives.

Attitudes

Once we got to Bible College, God didn't waste any time. He started right in with the area of my attitudes. Has God ever dealt with you through your being offended? Well, I was offended. Right or wrong, that first fall, I was offended.

For the first time in years, Chester and I had to abide by somebody else's rules, the Bible College rules. They were designed for eighteen to twenty-one-year-olds. We were told how to dress, what not to drink and where not to go. Learning Greek vocabulary was easy compared to having a sweet attitude in the face of a bunch of "rinky dink" rules. I found out that I had a rotten attitude.

"Lord, I think this is dumb. If this is Your plan, I don't like the small print. I am forty-three years old and don't need someone else telling me what to do."

For a week or two, I expected the Dean to wink at me and say that the rules were just for the younger students. That didn't happen.

As I was about to complain to the Lord again, He asked me,

"Betsy, do you want to understand authority?"

"Yes, Lord, of course."

"Then you must to learn to submit."

As I repented of my disgruntled attitude, I knew that God's help would be forthcoming. He sent much grace and my attitude changed quickly.

Bible Courses

We "studied to show ourselves approved."[1] We tried to fit in. We continued to trust God that we weren't too old to be useful and that someday, somewhere, somebody would want us.

As we began our Bible courses, God's wonderful Word penetrated our "beings," bringing revelation and life, changing us.

> Is not My Word like fire, declares the Lord and like a hammer that shatters a rock?[2]

We began with The Pentateuch, The Life of Christ and Greek. Each course brought, in addition to knowledge, clearer principles which we began to apply to our daily lives. Excitedly, we would interrupt each other while studying.

"Have you read that passage yet?" one of us would ask. "Just wait until you translate the crucifixion and the resurrection from the original Greek. It's tremendous."

Bible College was a privilege, a luxury and a necessity. How else could we prepare for whatever it was that God had ahead? We soaked in the rich teaching, as well as the excellent sermons by Teacher/Pastor Jim Darnell.[3] It was as if we each had a hidden reservoir that was slowly being filled.

---

[1] 2 Timothy 2:16
[2] Jeremiah 23:29
[3] He is now based in San Marcus, Texas.

Bible College
God's Multifaceted Approach

God's training plan for us had many dimensions. He wanted to touch our minds, our spirits and our emotions. He wanted to give us purpose and vision. He wanted to set us free from more of our life-long bondages. In the midst of our training, however, He did not neglect to encourage us.

"Trespassers"

In the spring of 1985, we heard that there was going to be a "Prophets Conference" in Fort Walton Beach, which was only an hour away. We were curious to find out more about these people called "prophets." The first night was to be for ministers only, yet we had been in Bible College for less than a year.

"Well, we're almost ministers," Chester insisted. "Lets go."

I agreed, hoping that we could get lost in the crowd. Arriving at Abundant Life Church, we were cordially welcomed and ushered into an upstairs room with about thirty-five other people. Our seats were right in the middle of the row. "No getting lost here!"

After worship and a short message, Dr. Bill Hamon and Randy Adler began to call out different couples and speak prophetically over them, simply speaking what they sensed the Lord was saying. I saw no way to leave without being extremely disruptive. My thoughts went like this:

"If this man really is a prophet, the first thing that God is going to tell him is that we are **not** ministers yet and that we **shouldn't** be here."

Shuddering , I awaited our time of exposure.

The first couple they prophesied to had been pastors for thirty-five years. They received an encouraging word. The next couple had been music leaders for eleven years. We were picked out next.

"It's all over," I thought, my imagination going wild.

The two men laid hands on us and Bishop Hamon began to speak to Chester.

> Well, God shows me that you have been involved in secular things and other things, but that you have laid on the floor and you've wept and you've cried and you've said, "God if I had only known sooner, I could have given myself so much sooner (to You)." The Lord says, I am the God who can redeem the time and I will do more with you in the last half of your life than if I had started even earlier with you. Because I knew you before you knew Me and I brought wisdom and maturity to you even when you didn't know that I was doing it.

I peeked over at Chester. Tears glistened on his cheeks. Everything this man was saying bore witness in his heart. Dr. Hamon continued:

> The Lord says that you have a strong teaching gift and that you will break the bread of life to many. Don't try to open any doors for yourself. God says, I will open the doors for you. Right now, just do what your hands find to do.

Amazing, absolutely amazing! What encouragement!

Bishop Hamon prophesied equally accurately concerning my life. Through him, the Lord addressed the unworthiness part of my dark side, the part that told me I could never measure up, that I would never qualify to serve God.

> Daughter, the Lord says to tell you that He doesn't call the qualified, **He qualifies the Called.**

This word was like a spear point that stabbed the heart of my self-depreciation. It was like a powerful wind that blew away a lot of my, "I am nots ..." and, "I can'ts ..." The dark side was continuing to lose!

God was telling me that I didn't have to measure up to some incredibly high standard that I thought He had set for me. I didn't have to try to be "qualified." He was telling me that He was in charge and that He would equip me with everything I needed to do His work. I felt like a ten-ton truck had just been driven off of my spirit.

Overwhelmed by God's goodness and by what had just happened, we went back to our seats. Ringing in our spirits, these gracious words confirmed that God planned to use us, especially in the teaching area and that we would bring His life to others. I was so excited that I forgot about the issue of being exposed as "trespassers."

Ministry Experiences

God's training program caused us to grow and develop in different ways. Our second year at Bible College, I was asked to teach several Christian Counseling courses. Chester was asked to teach a course on Science and the Bible. In addition, I went downtown to a women's ministry house for street people, to share a Bible study/devotional.

On Saturday mornings, I met for prayer with the young women in leadership at the college. I loved being part of their lives. Chester spent a semester ministering on Sunday nights at the local jail. Later we became Cell Group leaders and then elders in our church. Each experience provided a special facet of our development.

More Deliverance

I told God I wanted to be trained for ministry. I can't remember telling Him that I wanted to be "worked on," but, He didn't ask my permission.

One day, minding my own business, I was waiting in an office at the college to have some papers signed. Carol, the lady behind the reception desk, looked over at me and said,

"If you ever decide that you want to get rid of that demon of fear that has been harassing you for such a long time, I'll be happy to help you."

I was shocked. Was my demon so big and bad, (and even worse) so obvious, that even this unknown lady could see it? I felt like my underwear was showing, in the worst kind of way. I mumbled "Thank you," and let her know that I had experienced "some" fears and also had experienced one time of deliverance.

"I know," she said casually.

On the way home I wondered,

"What can one do to cover up his demons so they don't show in public?"

The following week, I decided to take advantage of Carol's offer. After inquiring, I found out that Carol and her husband Marvin were people of excellent reputation, known for their discernment and for helping people receive freedom from demonic forces. Chester went with me to my appointment with them and with Mary, their intercessor.

I told Carol about the deliverance Chester and I had previously experienced in the mountains. She explained that often it takes more than one deliverance to get complete freedom from something that has been a real stronghold in one's life. As she talked, I was getting more and more frightened. The tulips on her mantel were starting to get fuzzy. I was getting light headed.

"It's okay," Carol reassured me. "Fear is manifesting and that is what we want. It can't stay."

Everyone was praying.

"The demon of fear is in your 'house.' You need to take authority over it and command it out, in the name of Jesus."

I started commanding, but began choking. I couldn't breathe. A voice from inside of me spoke.

"I am going to kill you," it said. "I am going to strangle you and nobody is going to help you. They are going to think that you are just coughing as part of the deliverance, but I am going to **choke the life** out of you!"

My mind flashed back to the first deliverance that I had with Pat Brooks. I had left her house feeling that my old enemy, the fear of being killed, wasn't totally dealt with. It wasn't!

I was terrified. I was being choked to death! I was choking and gasping and no one was even patting me on the back, or getting me a drink of water. I tried to speak, to get them to stop before the demon killed me, but I was choking too much to talk! I was going to die!

At that moment, Mary, our intercessor, had a word of knowledge about something in my generational line that needed to be dealt with.

She said, "Your life really was threatened at one time. I don't understand it all, but there was a time when you could have died. Maybe there was a time when your birth mother considered aborting you."

In amongst the choking and coughing, I nodded my head in agreement that I forgave anyone who had threatened in any way to kill me. They had me specifically spoke forgiveness to my birth mother, whoever she might be.

As soon as this was accomplished, that powerful demon, that demon who had had the right to terrify me ever since I was a little girl, came out. I knew it instantly. It was gone.

The choking stopped and I had quietness inside, peace and victory. Weary but jubilant, I knew I was free. I knew the last part of my dark side had lost, was gone. "Lord, You have given me back my life!"

> ... that by [going through] death He might bring to nought *and* make of no effect him who had the **power of death**, that is the devil; and also that He might **deliver *and* completely set free all those** who through the (haunting) **fear of death** were **held in bondage** throughout the whole course of their lives.[1]

---

[1] Hebrews 2:14-15

Driving home that night, Chester and I stopped by Church's Chicken for a snack. Even though it was already past midnight, we were too excited to sleep. Not only was I free, something was birthed in us to see others set free from these same kind of life-defeating bondages. Spiritually, we were on our way to school with the "Green Berets."

Missions

God was not only setting us free, He was also changing our hearts. Every year, He stirred our hearts for missions. The great highlight of the college and church year was the Mission conference. Liberty Church Westside was a missions-spirited church and our missionaries were part of our lives. We signed up to have them stay in our homes, to include them for meals and to help support them for the coming year. Each year, around fifty of the hundred missionaries covered by Globe Missionary Evangelism came to the church to share their lives. Carrying the colorful flags of their nations, these fifty missionary families marched into church together, reminding all of us that God was on the move around the globe.

For five days, Chester and I would sit engrossed, listening to their accounts of family life, of new converts and of God's great miracles. Sometimes they honestly shared discouragement. Some were plowing hard ground. Some had to circumnavigate massive amounts of red tape just to minister where they were.

"God has given us the nations as our inheritance and we know that those from every tribe and nation will be at the marriage supper of the Lamb," they said, paraphrasing scripture.[1]

Our hearts burned, filled with the powerful urgency of getting the gospel message to all the nations.

"Lord, send us!" I cried. "We're not afraid to go."

I waited and waited for His still, small voice, for some impression that I could interpret as a "Yes." It never came. For now, His plans for us lay in another direction. The time to go overseas would come later.

---

[1] Psalm 2:8 and Revelation 19:5-9

Bible College
Lessons in Humility:
The Traffic Cop Is Fired

We spent much time wondering what we were going to do when we "grew up" and became "real ministers." I was envious of people who already knew what they were going to do. Meanwhile, we just had to go on with life and wait for further directions to come when the Lord was ready to give them. Meanwhile, too, we tried to pay the bills, keep the house gutters clean, be good parents to our children and good children to our parents. God was continuing to work on our lives.

It is an established fact that when God wants to get a point across, He will find a way to do it. After all, He used Balaam's donkey to confront him.[1] In my case, He used my family. It wasn't the sweet, "Mother, we all love you," kind of occasion. It was more like the lancing of a boil!

Christmas of 1986, our family was gathering in Pensacola, FL. I guess our "blended family" needed a few more minutes in the blender (on high), because things weren't too smooth. There was an underlying tension that seemed to increase with the addition of each family member who came back into our family circle.

Everyone was home: James, Lewis, Eric, Pam, Chester and myself. I had lofty hopes and aspirations.

"Lord, let us get through this Christmas without fighting with each other."

More exactly translated, this meant "without **them** fighting."

That year, I had thought of some nice dinner conversation topics, neutral enough for everyone to participate. I applauded myself.

---

[1] Numbers 22:28-33

With steaming vegetables on the table (someone in our family was always in a vegetarian phase) and the Christmas center-piece mostly intact, we sat down to enjoy our mealtime togetherness. As everyone finished being served, I was prepared to ease one of my selected topics into the mainstream conversation and watch it float. Before I could get the words out, however, one of our young adult children asked why there wasn't any salt on the table.

"I don't like my squash casserole without salt!"

My husband had been reading about the dangers of too much salt. I saw the frown starting to form on his brow. I knew a little mini-teaching would be forthcoming. It would be full of true facts and highly informative, but would also leave our "salt-seeker" in a state of agitation.

"Well you see," I jumped in, "we are switching to sea salt, which has so many benefits and there is some in the kitchen, if you want just a little sprinkle."

He brought the box out, set it on the table and put a layer of salt on the squash.

"Whew! Crisis averted," I thought.

Chester, however, had the look of someone who had been completely cut off, maybe even thrown into reverse without passing through neutral.

"Well," I said, trying to sound casual, "what do you think of the deliberations in Washington around cutting support for financial aid programs in colleges and universities?"

"Pass the potatoes, please."

"This squash is not bad."

Several takers on more vegetables, but none on financial aid.

Then one son asked another, "Are you dating anybody decent?"

"How can I with no car? I have to double date, or borrow a car if I go anywhere. What a drag, huh? Who wants to have a date on campus? Have you forgotten how deadly that is? Give me a break."

Everybody jumped in.

"Why don't you find a girl who likes to play chess?"

"Come on, you're creative."

Inside, my heart wrenched. Because we were in Bible College, all of our son's summer earnings had to go for his tuition, not for the much-wanted car. I felt the pain of his dilemma.

"I hope by next summer we will be able to help you with a car, so you can have some freedom," I intervened.

Inside I was thinking, "Why couldn't the others see that they were just making things worse, being so totally unsympathetic? After all, it doesn't take a sensitivity expert to validate that being stranded is no fun!"

That ended the dating conversation and there seemed to be an undefined gloom over our dinner table. Then our oldest son spoke up.

"Mom," he said, looking at me very intently, "I wish you would stop controlling our conversations. You're acting like a traffic cop, directing traffic. You're so afraid somebody is going to get hurt. Can't you just trust us enough to let us work it out?"

Another son chimed in. "Mom, I know you've been trying to help, but you are just interfering. You are not letting us get our 'stuff' out."

I was stunned. "What do you mean?"

I knew I was just trying my best to help. More than anything, I only wanted them all to be loving and sensitive to each other. I just wanted to have a little peace in our home. Trying not to show my hurt, I risked asking the gut-wrenching question.

"Do the rest of you also think I am controlling?"

For the next two hours, my somewhat blended family members offered me the plain facts. Their words, held in for so many years, contained overt frustration and irritation. They also contained the loss and sadness they felt over the way things were and the way things might have been, if only I could have let them be free and real with each other. The topic was opened

111

up. The need to talk it out won out over eating dinner and we left the half-finished meal, salty squash and all, and adjourned to the family room.

"Mom, you've got to let us be real with each other ..."

I knew they were right. "I will try," I said, wondering if I could do what they were asking.

For years, I had felt the overwhelming responsibility of trying to bring this family together, this family that always defied my best efforts. Now they were angry with me, totally unappreciative of my being their undercover agent, secretly working for their good.

I tried to get them to see my perspective. Then I realized a horrible thing. They **did** see it, but they still didn't like it and they didn't want it.

"Mom, can't you see that it is not working for us and it is not working for you either. You have got to stop controlling us, even if you think you are doing it for our good."

In my pain, my remaining dark side took over. I fell blindly into my old shame response.

"I'm just horrible and it's all my fault," I verbalized in so many words. Fortunately, they didn't buy that either.

"No, Mom, what you want is a good thing, but you are going about it in the wrong way. You're not bad, but your controlling all of us is not right. Can't you see that we love each other even when we disagree? Can't you give us space to work it out?"

Chester and my different children came and sat near me during that long, painful evening, touching my arm or patting my shoulder, reassuring me how much they cared. I couldn't hold back my tears. One AM came. We were all exhausted. We hugged and said, "Good night."

No one had cared about the government's financial aid program, but they did care enough about our family to address my control. Very shaken, the traffic cop walked back to her bedroom and took off her badge before getting into bed.

"Lord, what I thought I was doing 'for their good' was really control. I give up. I can't fix this family anyway. I give each one of them back to You; each one and all his relationships with the rest of us. Lord, would You like my badge?"[1]

---

[1] Dear reader, you must realize that responsible cops don't resign easily. In actuality, my "badge" had to be turned in on repeated occasions, as I turned over to the Lord "one more time" the monumental task of "fixing" my family. In answer to your question, "No, I am not perfect yet, but I am quick to recognize my 'nice' control, and on most days, quick to give it up."

Bible College
Lessons in Trust

"Why, Lord, is it so hard for me to live up to these two simple little verses?"

This was part of my ongoing conversation with the Lord. The scripture verses I was referring to were in Proverbs; Proverbs 3:5-6, to be exact. They say,

> Trust in the Lord with all your heart and do not lean to your own understanding. In all your ways acknowledge Him and He will make your paths straight.

Well, I don't know about your "own understanding," but mine likes to run things. It prefers to be the boss, to stay in charge. It is not at all fond of getting out of the way and being replaced by God's ways. (I'm sure mine worked closely with the traffic cop.) So many times I've prayed, "Lord, take my life," and then I've had so much trouble giving it to Him, trusting Him. During our Bible College years, God was teaching me more about trust. He knew we were going to need lots of it in the future.

One of the great things about trust is that it grows with usage. When we trust God and do things His way, we will see His faithfulness. The next time, it becomes just a little easier to trust Him. God provided many opportunities for my trust to grow.

God Provides

At one point, our money had shrink almost to zero. We had no jobs, no income.[1] Then He provided.

In 1985, we felt that God was saying to buy a house, but still neither of us had jobs.

"What kind of nuts will we look like when it comes out during the house closing that we're not even employed?" I wondered.

---

[1] See Chester's account of our financial testimony in Part 2.

114

"Just trust Me," the Lord said.

Guess what? We were never questioned about our jobs. The Realtor only checked our credit rating (which was excellent) and we purchased the house. Soon afterwards, our jobs came through.

Nina

The fall of our third year, when I thought our trust had grown quite enough, thank you, we had another time of testing. We received an unexpected bill from Davidson College for our son, Lewis. It was for $4,500 and was due in three weeks. After calling the college, we realized that we had misunderstood the nature of his scholarship. It turned out that it was "need" based as well as academically based.

God had so provided for us the previous year that the college grant committee decided Lewis no longer "needed" the entire scholarship. (The fact that Chester was once again fully in Bible College and not employed was not their consideration and rightly so. We had just not understood and therefore not planned for this.)

We had a few hundred dollars in the bank and were aghast. "Lord, help!" This time we needed mountain-moving faith.

As we left our home to go to a friend's beach house to pray, our son Eric asked us if we would mind praying for his friend Nina in Thailand, since we were going to pray anyway.

"Sure, why not?" we replied, very much engrossed in our own crisis.

Shortly after arriving, I began with one of my now famous "911" prayers.

"Help, Emergency, come immediately! Lord, there's been a misunderstanding. We are in trouble!" I began. "Lord, how have we missed it? What should we do now?"

We poured our hearts out to the Lord for a while, with no response. It felt like our prayers were bouncing off of the ceiling. After a while, discouraged, we decided to take a break. Want-

115

ing to honor our promise, I suggested we pray for Eric's friend Nina. We did know a little about her, but not much. We knew that Nina had been in Eric's circle of friends at Asbury College and she had returned to her home in Thailand after graduation.

Chester and I prayed separately, silently. The Lord spoke to my heart.

"You are to invite Nina to come here, have her live in your home and help her go to Bible College."

I was shocked. "Lord, You've got to be kidding! You don't understand. It's us. Remember? We're the ones who are having the crisis. We are the couple who already have **too many** children and **too much** college. That's why we are here!"

Lacking the fortitude to share this piece of news with Chester, I instead sweetly asked him,

"Chester, has God said anything to you?"

Chester repeated exactly what I had just heard, plus the fact that we were to pay Nina's airfare from Thailand and her way to Bible College. Then he added,

"God says she will be as a daughter to us."

We sat dumbfounded and stared at each other, with tears in our eyes.

It was so unusual, so impossible, so amazing, that it had to be God. We couldn't have made it up. We tried to pray some more. We wanted the Lord to tell us just how He was going to take care of the tuition crisis and help us with Nina. All He seemed to be saying was, "Just Trust Me."

Somehow we both knew that the Lord wouldn't be asking us to provide for another "child," unless He was going to help us take care of the ones that we already had. To us, that definitely meant providing for Lewis.

"Lord, we don't see how You are going to do it, but we trust You."

That night, we had Eric call Nina in Bangkok. He introduced us over the phone and we explained to her what had happened.

She could hardly believe it. After a long silence, she explained to us that she had been fasting and praying for two weeks, asking God to provide her a scholarship to a Bible College somewhere!

"Now," she said, "you must pray that my father will let me come."

We agreed to pray and write to him and said, "Good-bye."

During the next ten months, so many things happened in Nina's life. Her father agreed for her to come the following fall. A piece of property her family had been trying to sell for ten years was sold. People began to ask her to tutor them in English.

When we called to arrange for her airfare the following spring, Nina said they had more than enough money to pay for it and it wasn't necessary for us to help.

In August, our new daughter arrived. She was spunky, had a wonderful sense of humor and desired to be a help to us. She was beautiful in appearance and deeply committed to the Lord.

The second day she was in our home, she handed Chester an envelope saying, "Here, Papa, this is for you."

It contained all of her tutoring money—over $3,000. We were overwhelmed, to say the least. We helped her open a bank account for the money and had her use it for her tuition, books and spending money. Again, God had provided. All we had to provide was her room and food to eat.

A year and a half later, she graduated from Liberty Bible College with her Master's Degree. Six months after that, she "officially" became our daughter, when she married our son, Eric.

It would take another chapter to tell you all the ways money came in to cover Lewis' college tuition. Just "trust" us, it did come in. Every penny that was needed got to Davidson College on time. We did not have to borrow from friends or family, or take out a loan. God provided!

I read an anonymous quote once which went like this.

Someday, some simple soul is going to come along and just believe that what the Bible says is true. That soul will be greatly blessed.

We were getting a little closer to that kind of trust.

Bible College
Our Ministry Folds
and Then Unfolds

Late in 1985, we met with Brother Ken Sumrall, the president of our Bible College and the founder of Liberty Ministries. We went to present to him a plan for training and equipping church people to counsel each other, using an effective format the Lord had been showing us.

All of the elements that would later make up Christian Prophetic Prayer Counseling were there in embryonic form. There was an emphasis on forgiveness, the need for ministry to Sins of the Fathers and resulting Curses, a procedure to change Ungodly Beliefs into Godly Beliefs, ministry to Soul/Spirit Hurts and the deliverance from Demonic Oppression. The seed form of the "Integrated Approach to Ministry" was present.

Brother Ken graciously gave his support and over the next two years, we were able to teach two eight-week classes; the first in 1986 and the second one in 1987. The insights and counseling approach we presented were received with great excitement.

After teaching the classes, we began to train husband-wife teams using Jesus' model of "on the job" training. I also matched counselees with the new teams. The counseling was beginning to bear fruit. There were others in the church doing counseling as well as ourselves, but in a church of twelve hundred, the need was great. Before long, our counseling program was turning into a half-time job.

The only problem was that there wasn't any "half time" left in our lives to give to it. Here we were attending Bible College, while Chester worked full-time in the aerospace industry. I was teaching classes in the Bible College. Our little counselor training program was about to take us over.

Even though we were overwhelmed, something was birthed in our spirits. We had talked about the power of God's freedom the night of my final deliverance from fear and now, we were seeing other people receive the same wonderful freedom. We were also learning a tremendous amount.

"Lord, there are so many wounded soldiers in Your Church. Is this the direction that You are calling us to move in?"

For the first time, God's answer came back a resounding, "YES!"

Our counseling mentoring continued for almost two years, then something happened. Our church had a change in pastors.

Suspicion

The new Senior Pastor didn't seem to trust us or the counseling model we were using. He didn't really know us and the model was unfamiliar to him. We were suspect. He called for an "investigation" to check us out, as well as the other counselors in the church.

We gave what we felt was a good scriptural defense of each area of the counseling. There were several meetings, but at the end, no concluding statements were made by our "investigators."

During that process, however, something died within me. The desire to teach, raise up counseling teams and see people ministered to, was squashed. Gone was the joy associated with the weeks and months of activities that had borne so much fruit.

Chester warned me not to take it so personally. My head listened, but my heart did not.

We had begun to have a vision for a Spirit-led counseling ministry. We believed it was a major way that the Lord wanted to use us in the future.

Now, suddenly, it was gone. I didn't understand. I was just hurt. Being mistrusted struck at the very core of my old "belonging" and "right to exist" issues. There was obviously still room for more healing.

I also didn't understand the concept of the death of a vision and that many times God calls us to put our vision, our child of promise, our Isaac, on His altar. Then we must leave it in His hands to raise it up, or not.

Although we never mentioned the "investigation" to the counseling teams, there was a supernatural dispersal of them. One moved to a new job, one adopted a baby, another had a time of work overload, and on it went. Over a two-month period, everything came to a screeching halt.

"Lord, we lay it all down. No more counseling program."

Two more years passed, years that included a sense of loss, hurt and confusion. Then, within the space of a few weeks, our "counseling shambles" began to be reframed by new understanding.

Resurrection

First, a visiting missionary spoke at the Bible College Chapel about the "Death of a Vision." He used Joseph's life as an illustration, pointing out how Joseph's great vision of ruling was followed by betrayal, accusation and prison.

I began to think of Moses and others. "Lord, this same thing that has happened to us also happened to men that You used greatly. Why hadn't I seen this before?"

There was more understanding several weeks later, as we were attending a Friday night School of the Holy Spirit at Christian International (about two hours from Pensacola). Kathy Webster, now a dear friend, gave us a prophetic word:

> I see that there was a time you were soaring like two sea gulls out over the ocean, having so much fun. But then God brought you back to shore. Right now, you are walking on the shore, unsure what to do next. God has you here while He is making some final preparations. There is going to come a time when you two will fly again. You will fly higher than before and this time you will not come back to the shore.

No one needed to interpret this for us. For the first time, we re-alized that the shutting down of the counseling program had been the Hand of the Lord. It was for His purposes. He would raise it up again.

Even further confirmation of our counseling ministry came sev-eral months later in July, 1988, at a conference led by Pastors Travis and Ann Thigpen held at Liberty Church Westside. Travis laid hands on us and with his wonderful, resonant voice began:

> For the Lord says, my son and my daughter, I have called you to be Repairers of the Breach, the people who are called to restore the waste places and to bring forth the anointing in the lives of others. For the Lord says, I've not just called you to repair lives, but I the Lord God have called you also to take them a step fur-ther and that is to release the anointing in their lives. Release them, says the Lord God, not just to successful life, but also to successful ministry.

> The Lord says, I the Lord God will do it much more in days to come. And the Lord says, you will see my hand and you will behold my face and you will see the very presence of my angels in the counseling room and office.

> And the Lord says, my son and my daughter, you will not just minister to couples and the Lord says, you will not just minister to individuals and the Lord says, you won't just teach in the classroom. The Lord says, I will open conferences for you. And the Lord says, I will send you out and you will go out, and come back, and go out and come in, go out and come in, go out and come in, and yet go out and come in again. And the Lord says, I will begin to cause people to know your name and the Lord says, they will know that you are a man and a woman of God. They will know that you're prophetic people who are able to hear my voice, move in my power, hear my principles and put them forth

with clarity of purpose and mind. And the Lord says, you will be ones that move in the gifts, and I'll give you great discernment, says the Lord, and I will give you a prophetic word.

As the Lord spoke through Travis, He breathed resurrection life into the two of us and into what we once thought was our ministry vision.

"Lord, it was You, after all."

Is There Life After Bible College?

Our ministry vision was validated and resurrected, which was great, but we felt "all dressed up with no place to go." Such excitement, such anticipation, but, "How, Lord and where?"

In the fall of 1988, we took our pop-up tent camper (which "popped up" most of the time) over to Sandestin, on the Gulf Coast of Florida. We wanted to attend a conference at Christian International (henceforth referred to as "CI"). On this trip we met Pastors Buddy and Mary Crum, who pastored a church in Dunwoody, Georgia, a suburb of Atlanta. The Crums were about our age and both had business backgrounds. We felt an immediate kinship with them.

"Why don't you come to see us some weekend and share your ministry vision?" they offered.

Early in 1989, we sat in their church office explaining in the most tentative way what we "thought, **perhaps**, that **maybe**, the Lord **might possibly**, be preparing us for."

Pastor Mary kept laughing. Just as I was thinking how foolish we must be sounding, she explained what was happening.

The Lord was showing her "the big picture" of our future, which by comparison made all of our hesitation sound a little ridiculous.

We shared that we wanted to "raise up the saints for the work of the ministry,"[1] the very thing they were already doing successfully in the prophetic area.

"We think it could work," they said.

We talked details. It was obvious that these Pastors were really excited about the potential of lay people becoming God's instruments of healing through prophetic counseling. We left, agreeing to stay in touch and with that warm satisfaction of feeling understood. They had caught the vision.

---

[1] Ephesians 4:12

First Ministry Opportunity

A year later, in January of 1990, we began training the first three lay counseling teams at Life Center Church. It was strenuous.

We would attend or teach Bible College classes Monday through Wednesday in Pensacola; drive to Atlanta on Thursday; counsel, train and teach class all weekend; and then drive back Sunday evening. We did this every other weekend for five months.

It helped to have some very dynamic people to work with and we all were energized about getting the program launched. The Crums provided friendship and guidance to us, with wise oversight at crucial decision points along the way. (Life Center now has a flourishing, self-reproducing counseling program that is greatly benefiting their people.)

Painful Preparation

That same year (1989) had been a heartbreaking time for our home church. Since it is not my intention to judge the events and decisions that were made, let me just say that the church went through a devastating split. One week things were normal, the next week, people were gone. Over the following three years, this church of 1200 decreased to 150 people. Many of the people that had been our extended family left. Our hearts were broken.

Early one morning, soon after the split, Chester called me into the bedroom where he was praying.

"I'm not sure what all this means," he confided, "but the Lord is telling me that we need to finish our school work and graduate from Bible College by this next spring. He is saying for us not to delay, that within two years the Bible College will be closed."

I could hardly believe it. The Bible College would close? We had planned to finish sometime in the near future, but immediately?

Finishing

I discontinued my part-time job as Liberty Church's counselor to women so that I could prepare to write. We each had a master's thesis to produce. Chester took all of the teaching notes from our lay counseling training classes and used them as the basis for his thesis. I wrote mine on, "A Christian Approach to Counseling a Homosexual," an area in which I had already done a lot of reading and some ministry. Just as I was getting started, God gave me the key to finishing my thesis:

"Put your seat on the chair in the morning and don't get up until evening."

We both finished just in time for spring graduation in 1990. Our children gathered from the four corners of the earth and cheered as we graduated. We cheered too. These had been six of the most important years of our lives.

The Bible College, which for so many years had been effectively training pastors and missionaries, closed its doors the following spring. God had truly been leading us.

Healing

As our church fell apart and the college closed, we needed to use everything we knew about God's healing for ourselves. We grieved over the turmoil and wreckage. We tried to forgive, asked forgiveness and went to the Lord with our pain. It was a time when no one else could be much help to us, because all of us were hurting in the same way.

Over the weeks and months the Lord spoke to our hearts many times. He reminded us that no matter what church leaders did, that He was still the same,[1] that He still "works all things together for good."[2] Sometimes, He just reassured us of His love, but He always let us know,

"I'm still in control of your lives. I am still leading you. Don't look to men, look to Me."

---

[1] Hebrews 13:8
[2] Romans 8:28

He provided the comfort we so greatly needed. Gradually, our wounds healed. Several years later the leaders, whose disagreements had caused the church split, reconciled publicly.

Continued Ministry Opportunity

The winter of 1991, we returned to Life Center Church. This time the church rented an apartment for us. With the help of our first group of teams, we spent several productive months of concentrated time training a second group of counselors. In the process we bonded strongly with the counseling teams, the church and its pastors. God had chosen the right place to launch us into the ministry.

Nothing Wasted

When the day came to leave Life Center and let the new teams "season" for a while, I reminded the Lord that we had no job and no place to go. The rented furniture was being taken out and only our suitcases and the phone were left. I reached to unplug it, but felt an impression to leave it a little longer. Within fifteen minutes, it rang.

"Hello, this is Ronnie. I am trying to pastor a church here in Texas that is having a crisis. There is a church situation here that I want to talk to you about and see if you can come help us with some counseling. Can you come for a year. How soon do you think you might be able to come?"

"This afternoon!" I felt like saying. It was useless to try to sound cool. I was overjoyed. I listened to the very sad scenario of events that had prompted his call.

"Yes, Pastor Ronnie, we will be happy to pray about it and get back with you. You really do need some help there. Call you in a few days. Good bye."

"Chester, how would you like to go to Texas for a year?" I asked, all smiles.

Texas

We arrived in a large city in Texas just after the fourth of July. There we loved much, counseled much, taught much and called back much to Life Center to ask for prayer. We, and the church, needed it.

The church we had come to serve had been devastated by a pastoral adultery situation. The adultery involved the pastor and the main church counselor. It had occurred over a period of eight years. These two people were greatly loved and had been instrumental in helping almost all of the members of that congregation through difficult times. Pastor Ronnie had been brought in as an interim pastor to help see the church through until it stabilized.

As we joined them for our first Wednesday night church service, some people were sitting there openly crying. Grief and despair filled the atmosphere. These people had been deceived and they were devastated. About two hundred people had already left the church, so that their past sense of family was destroyed.

Our hearts were touched. Only two years earlier, we had experienced a church split within our home church. We knew how it felt. Putting our notes aside, we began to share from our hearts. Although the external circumstances had been quite different, the feelings, the shattering, the sense of overwhelming loss was the same. We knew one important thing. If God could heal us (and He had), He could also heal them!

"I have come to heal the brokenhearted," Jesus declared of Himself, "to set at liberty those who are bruised."[1]

"Lord," we prayed, "come and do it once again. Come and heal the hearts of Your people." We knew that God had sent us to the right place.

When a pastor falls, threat and disillusionment come like waves over the people. Silently they ask the faith-shattering question, "If the man of God can't make it, what hope do I have that I can make it?"

Key Revelation
Everybody needed help. "Lord, what shall we do?"

"Minister to them all at the same time," came back the answer. "I will heal them."

"Fine, Lord, but how exactly do we do that?" we wondered.

Then He began to show us that we could minister to the whole church the same way that we would to an individual! For example, we needed to allow them time for forgiveness and repentance. Then we could lead them through the same four ministry areas that He had shown us were necessary for individuals.

---

[1] Luke 4:18

129

He opened our eyes to see that there were Sins of the "Founding" Fathers and Curses coming out of the pastor's sin, as well as from the other founding leaders; that church-wide Ungodly Beliefs had been formed; that every member had suffered similar Soul/Spirit Hurts; and that in the area of Demonic Oppression, there were specific spirits over the church that were affecting everybody. For us, this was a powerful revelation.

Over the rest of the summer and through the fall, we taught and ministered, while God did an amazing amount of healing. It was not all of the healing that was needed, but with the Lord's help, we all crossed a threshold; the church turned around and began the healing process.

Praying for Strategy
The Lord was showing us that He had the battle plan, His strategy, both for an individual and for a church. Our job was to seek Him and to work with His plan. Although we always prayed for a strategy before a counseling session, it sometimes wasn't revealed until after we started the session. He never failed, however, to show us what to do. He revealed how to disassemble a stronghold, or when to simply pray and wait. As in all the amazing events of our lives, He continued to lead us.

Supervision Important
During the year we were in Texas, we continued to go every six weeks to Life Center in Atlanta to train and oversee the lay counseling teams. We would "sit in," observe a counseling session and then give the team feedback. We believe this is the most effective way to provide supervision and to help counseling teams continue to mature.

Reproducing Reproducers
In the winter of 1993, we came to Atlanta for one final round of training. We not only had the previously trained teams help us train the new teams, we taught the teams how to conduct the classroom teaching and how to train new teams. At the end of this time, Charles and Jackie Clifton, a wonderfully anointed Life Center team, were ready to move into our place as oversight team. Confidently, we handed them the reins.

We walked away feeling very much like we were leaving our home and our children, but we knew that for now, our job there was completed. Pastors Buddy and Mary prayed for us that last Sunday:

> Now the foundation has been laid. You have been faithful and God is about to open many doors for you. God is going to use Christian International (the next place that we were going) as a launching pad, because what He has given to you, He wants to take to the world. The time of your launching is at hand.

"Take to the world, Lord? Chester and me? You want to take what You have given us all over the world?"

Then I remembered Charles Browning's words to us ten years earlier.

> The Lord says that there are people waiting in different parts of the world for you to bring your message.

We felt both ready and not ready for what God had ahead. Excited, yes; confident, no. As He was getting us ready "to launch," a most precious healing was about to occur, a healing that would blow away the last dreary shadows of my dark side.

More Healing
The Long Awaited "Thank You"

There they were again, my private collection of stillborn "Thank-yous." Why didn't they just go away and leave me alone? In my mind's eye, I had a whole drawer of thank-you notes, each one written at a different time and season of my life, as maturity and fresh realizations came. These were all thank-yous to an unknown woman, living at an unknown address, or maybe not living at all. Many times, I had tried to empty out this drawer, but somehow the notes always found their way back in. I carried a deep desire to say "Thank-you" to this unknown woman, my flesh and blood birth mother.

Mixed Feelings
At first, I battled within myself. I didn't understand my own feelings. After all, I had very exceptional parents. I loved them, respected them, enjoyed them, and visa versa. I couldn't have asked for more.

Toward the end of their lives, I experienced deep sadness, knowing that times with them were fleeting away. I cherished our special moments together. Chester and I made sacrifices so I could have these treasured times. As the spaces of their lives narrowed, I found joy in the little things, in our history, a laugh over hospital food, or simply in caring for them.

In spite of this totally fulfilling love, my "Thank-you" drawer would not stay empty. At times, I felt like turning cartwheels and hollering exuberantly to that unknown woman; "Thank-you for my life. It's been so good, so rich, so hard at times, yet so full."

One note to her said, "Thanks for enduring the shame and disgrace of having an illegitimate baby in 1940. Thanks for the generous decision you made to let me have a chance in life. I've been so blessed."

132

Another note was written during my childbearing years, when my own two sons were born. It said, "The joy of holding my beautiful babies in my arms is helping me to forget how much my bottom hurts. They are so wonderful, so perfect in every way. It's more than worth the pain. But today, I am thinking of you. Oh, 'Thank-you,' nameless woman, for your once sore bottom, empty arms and aching heart. All of that pain and nothing to show for it. I so hope that you had healthy babies to love and to sing to; babies to grow up and fulfill your mother's heart."

Then there were a few notes written on October 5, my birthday.

"I am celebrating today," the note said. "Always there has been a party for me: a surprise party once, a slumber party another time and a movie party. Once, when I was five, I had a party to which I only invited boys. I always feel so special on my birthday. There is, however, one little missing piece. In some way, this is our day. You were the only one who was there. I can't help but wonder if you are thinking of me today, or if you've long since blanketed your pain and allowed the fact that you had a baby girl to become only a faded memory. If you have had a silent wondering, asking yourself if you made a mistake to let me go, please know that you did the right thing, the best thing for us both. Please forgive yourself any way that you need to, but know, nameless woman, that I am thanking you. You will always have a special place in my heart. However you feel, I still bless you and thank you every October 5."

There was also another note that said, "Send with Caution" on the envelope. This one contained the hard questions about the circumstances of my conception and the issues that I was trying to work through about my value. This was the only one lacking a "Thank-you."

Yes, these were some of the numerous notes that filled my private drawer. They couldn't be sent because there was nowhere to send them. Nevertheless, they were the intimate reflections of my heart.

Difficult Area

Over the years, my mother Betty, who spoke so straightfor-
wardly about everything else, would speak only indirectly about
my birth roots. She was not entirely comfortable with this area,
particularly with the idea of my doing any "investigation." As
open and as close as I was with her, and as much as I hated hid-
denness, it seemed to me that talking about my "Thank-you"
drawer would only cause needless pain. I chose not to do it. I
think it was best.

My greatest conversations about my birth mother were with the
Lord.

"Lord," I prayed on more than one occasion, "please keep her
safe, if she is alive. Please bless her family, if she has one.
Lord, most of all, please tell her 'Thank-you' for me."

Several times over the years, I questioned the Lord about trying
to find her, but I always sensed, "Just wait."

Right Timing

It was September, 1993. My precious mother Betty had died a
month earlier, pneumonia being the final cause that overcame
her bright spirit and frail body.

I missed her greatly. I reflected on our brief conversation the
night before she died.

"I just feel awful," she said, never mincing words. "I didn't
know a body could feel this bad. They're coming into my room
with some oxygen now, but for goodness sake, don't worry
about me. I always pull through these things."

"I love you, Mother."

"Yes, I love you too."

This time, however, she didn't pull through. My mother, precious to me beyond words, was gone. She had been so bubbling with the enjoyment of life, yet never sentimentalizing its
shortcomings; so full of shrewd observations, occasionally a little too critical, yet kind and always lovingly there for me. How
I would miss her!

It was a month later in my quiet time that the thought suddenly struck me.

"Lord, You remember about my 'Thank-you' notes? Is it okay, now? Do I have permission to look for my birth mother?" This time, unlike all of the other times, I sensed a resounding "Yes!"

I Initiate

Crash! Boom! It was as if my private drawer came flying out, crammed full of a lifetime's worth of notes, all waiting to be sent.

"What if she is not alive?" I half whispered to myself.

Through the years, I had only once contacted the North Carolina Children's Home Society in Greensboro, the agency through which I had been adopted. They were helpful and extremely sensitive to my situation, but legally not at liberty to give me the information that would help me trace my roots. So I contacted an Adoption Search Consultant, mailing her copies of my birth certificate. Her words to me contained both wisdom and caution.

"Are you prepared to face anything, even severe rejection? That sometimes happens, you know."

"Yes, I have thought about that possibility many times," I reassured her. "I believe that I am prepared."

The consultant then let me know that even if the birth parents were no longer living or were very negative, she was usually able to locate some of the relatives.

"I'll call you as soon as I know anything," she said cheerfully, sounding as if it were an everyday occurrence.

Three days later my phone rang.

"I have some good news for you," she said. "Not only is your birth mother living, but you have the best possible chance of having her talk with you."

"Why is that?" I queried.

"Well, her spouse is deceased, so if she never told him, she wouldn't be in a dilemma. Many birth parents never share their secret with their spouses."

"Oh, I see." I had never thought about these issues.

"Are you ready for her name?"

Her name? Her name! How many times had I wondered what her name was.

"Her name is Virginia and she lives in Virginia Beach."

"Virginia. Virginia." Rapidly, I thought of all of the Virginias that I had known, probably half a dozen. All of my associations were positive.

The consultant went on to give me information about Virginia's three sons; their names, addresses and phone numbers.

For fifty-three years she had been a nameless woman. Now, in an instant of time, she had become "Virginia."

"Oh, Virginia, who are you?" I wondered.

My consultant proceeded with some excellent advice.

"Remember, it is going to be a big shock to her to hear from you. She could have a room full of children or grandchildren. Ask her if it is a convenient time to talk to her. Tell her that you have something personal that you want to say."

That made sense, but never would I have come up with the approach which she next suggested.

"If she can talk, give her your birth date and where you were born. Ask her if that means anything to her. That will leave the ball in her court. Let me know how it turns out. Good luck now."

I felt somewhat protected knowing that my consultant had been helping people find their birth parents for over fifteen years and was a birth mother herself, who had gone through the process of finding her own daughter.

Chester prayed with me again and I picked up the phone to call. Shaking too much to stand, I sat down to steady myself. All of my "what ifs" stampeded through my mind.

"What if you were the child of rape or incest and she hates you? What if she says your birth date means nothing? What if she hangs up rudely, or just as bad, tells you in a polite, pinched voice to never call again? Are you really ready to face that? Then what will you do with all of your 'Thank-yous'?"

As quickly as the stampede came, it passed on by and was replaced by a very familiar, recognizable peace.

"Yes, Lord. I know that You will be with me, no matter what happens."

How many times has He reassured me that I was not alone?

Virginia

My first encounter was with Virginia's answering machine. This older woman's voice ended her soft-spoken message with, "Have a good day. God bless you."

Excitement hit, like waves pounding on the sand. I called every ten minutes for the next hour. Finally, I heard an "alive" voice.

"Hello," she answered pleasantly, but soon sounded almost disoriented as I asked if it were a convenient time to talk with her.

"Who is this?" was the question in her voice.

"Virginia, does October 5, 1940, Durham, North Carolina, mean anything to you?" I asked, trying to control my voice. A long silence followed, a very long silence.

"Lord, don't let her hang up," I pleaded silently.

Slowly, she responded. "You could only be one person," she said. "I want you to know that I have prayed for you every day of your life. I gave you up because I loved you so much. I wanted you to have things that I knew I couldn't give to you."

I couldn't speak. "Thank-you," I said after awhile. "Thank-you."

137

Virginia and I talked for two hours. Between us, we had one hundred twenty-three years to catch up on. Where to start?

I began almost demographically, sharing that I had been raised in a wonderful home, had been through an early divorce, had two sons and that I had been married to Chester for almost twenty years. I also told her of my stepchildren and that Chester and I were in ministry, though not giving any details.

"That is so wonderful," she said, audible relief in her voice. "I am so thankful. I have been so concerned about you. I tried three times to find you, but could never get any specific information. I always felt sad on your birthday and even on Christmas, thinking about you."

Then she began to give me the details of her life, her family, teen years, my birth, her marriage and four children.

"Four?" I questioned.

"Yes," she said. "I have three sons; Joey, Mickey and Mark, and also a daughter named Connie."

As Virginia talked about her children and grandchildren, I could hear her care and involvement with them, her mother's heart.

"I hope I get to meet them," I commented. This was especially true of Connie. I had always wanted a sister.

"She doesn't know about you," Virginia went on. "None of my children do. I felt it was wiser not to tell them unless I was able to find you."

I understood.

Virginia told me about her husband Joe, who had been a civil engineer. He had helped design and oversee several of the major bridges around Norfolk and Virginia Beach. I could hear the pride in her voice as she spoke of him. Joe had died of cancer several years before.

"He would have been so excited about meeting you," she added.

Then the focus came back to the different kinds of work she had done, especially about her work at a psychiatric hospital as a receptionist.

"There is one thing that I always wanted to do," she said with a hint of regret in her voice, "but I didn't have the opportunity."

I was curious now. "What was that?" I asked.

"I always wanted to be a counselor."

I couldn't believe it! I started laughing and crying as the impact hit. I understood.

"Let me tell you about my life," I interrupted, still almost unable to believe what she was saying. "I think that I started counseling when I was about seven-years old!"

Now it was her turn to laugh, which she did as I traced my love of counseling through its history of numerous positions, jobs, degrees, Bible College teaching and current involvement in a counseling ministry. Across the years of unknowns, a bonding was taking place.

I asked about my birth father.[1] Yes, she had loved him, but she was only sixteen and he nineteen at the time she became pregnant.

"It's best that I didn't marry him," she said, giving her own personal reasons. I knew that she meant it. "He did contribute money for your birth. He is married and lives in our home town."

"You know," she said, "when you turned fifty and had never tried to contact me, I gave up on ever knowing you. I felt terribly sad."

"Thank-you," I said again, not minding if I sounded a little redundant. At last, without restraint, I had the joy of speaking my "thank-yous" out loud. I felt as if my heart, as well as my secret drawer, was being emptied out.

---

[1] I contacted my birth father and had a pleasant conversation, but he was not open to an ongoing relationship out of concern for his wife.

Rocking Chairs

Virginia and I talked about the Lord and about our faith. We talked about times that each of us had known His nearness. The night before I had made contact with Virginia, I had been awake almost all night just thinking about her. I had sat in my rocking chair, praying and writing as I so often do. That same night, she had not been able to sleep either. She had felt a strange restlessness, her signal to get up and pray.

"I couldn't decide who I was supposed to pray for," she admitted, "and the only person that seemed to fit was your birth father. I am not sure that he knows the Lord. So I got up and sat in my little rocking chair in my living room and prayed once again for him and for you."

I smiled to think about it. There we were, several states apart, totally unknown to each other, sitting in our respective rocking chairs, praying for each other at the same time!

As she told me the content of her prayers for me over the years, I realized how many had been answered; prayers for my health and safety, prayers for my happiness and even for my salvation. In lots of ways, my prayers for Virginia had been answered too.

There was so much to think about. I was weary with emotion.

My nameless woman had a name and was very much alive. She was a woman of integrity and also of prayer. In her silent way, she had loved me all these years. She even had a counselor's heart!

"Thank-you," I said one final time after we hung up, just for the joy of saying it and because I had a lot of new things to be thankful for. At long last, my drawer of secret "Thank-yous" was empty, but my heart was full. God had done another step in bringing about His healing.

Launching

As I described earlier, Chester had worked several years at Cape Kennedy as part of the US Air Force rocket launch team. It is interesting that many times when the Lord has spoken to us through prophetic people, rocket imagery has been used.

"I see you on the launch pad, but the rocket is not ready to be fired," one said, back in our Bible College days.

A few years later a different prophet in another setting said, "God says, don't try to launch too soon. Wait for Him to light the fuse."

The next year another prophet said, "God says, 'Get ready, I'm lighting the fuse. This is the time of launching.'"

Not a lot happened for a while after that, so we decided our rocket must have either a very long fuse, or a slow-burning one!

Then Pastors Buddy and Mary again used that rocket imagery. "The time of launching is at hand."

Once we arrived at CI in the spring of 1993, things started happening so fast and furiously that I turned to Chester one day overwhelmed and said,

"I think our rocket has been launched! It is zooming through space at a horrendous speed and I feel as if I am being dragged along behind the rocket, holding on for dear life. I don't think that we are running this thing!"

Assignment at CI

Dr. Bill Hamon, the founder of Christian International Ministries, had asked us to come and counsel himself and his wife, his leadership and Board of Governors. With the wisdom and humility that has characterized his life, he said,

"I believe that God is saying that as a ministry we have reached a plateau; we have gone as far as we can go. I also believe that with personal ministry, it will be possible for us corporately to break through to a higher level."

We agreed to come.

Bishop Hamon had checked us out, first through Pastors Buddy and Mary Crum, and then by having us counsel one of his key leadership couples, Scott and Kathy Webster.

He chose the right couple! They were open and ready to receive all that the Lord had for them through the counseling. Not only did their lives begin to change and their children's lives change, but they also became advocates for the prophetic counseling ministry. In their own unpretentious way, they paved the way for our coming to CI.[1]

Arriving at CI, we began counseling, full steam ahead. At the same time, under the leadership of Pastors Tom and Jane Hamon, we were raising up three lay counseling teams to minister within the CI Family Church. "Our plate was quite full." Then we were approached again.

"We think you should just do a little workshop during the conference and present an overview of your counseling approach."

And then later: "It would be good for you to do an afternoon session during the September Prophetic Intensive Training."

Then that fall Bishop Hamon said,

"I think you two need to do a Prophetic Counseling Conference for us next spring. Its time to share what God has shown you with others on a broader scale. I think that we will have a

---

[1] Their loving friendship has been and continues to be very significant in our lives.

number of people that will want to hear what you have to share." He talked as if it were settled.

We discussed how we had been wanting to write a training manual covering the Christian Prophetic Prayer Counseling topics and that maybe this was the time. He agreed that it would be helpful to give it out to the people attending so they would have something to take home with them. We decided go ahead with the writing project, along with planning the seminar. We knew that we faced another time of "stretching!"

First Conference

Come the following March, in 1994, we had our first conference. It was really more like a family production.

Gary and Sharon Potter helped us coordinate arts presentations with our teaching, for a powerful synergistic effect. Scott and Kathy Webster gave their testimony about going through their counseling. Many of the staff couples that we had counseled, along with teams we had trained at other churches, came and helped minister to the audience. Looking out and seeing the faces of so many of our friends, I felt like all of CI was behind us, pulling for us, praying for us, helping us through this "birthing."

"Is there anything that you need, Mrs. Betsy?" Jimmy Kellet would ask affectionately.

No, there wasn't, because everybody was already doing it. Bishop and Mom Hamon were sitting on the front row beaming. It was a very precious gift to have an entire ministry behind us.

We had worked very hard and managed to finish a "preliminary version" of *Restoring the Foundations* in time to hand out a copy to every conference participant. We were able to present in a comprehensive way all of the basic counseling revelations and understandings the Holy Spirit had given us, both in ministering healing through counseling and in raising up new counseling teams.

Many lives were touched by God's healing power during that conference. God used it to open wide the door of His plans and purposes for us, that we might have many more opportunities to minister to the Body of Christ. Chester and I were no longer on the rocket pad. God had truly launched us.

Our greatest need ahead was going to be absolute trust and confidence in Him; in His plans for us, in His timing, in His financial provision. For almost ten years, the Lord had been preparing us, teaching us step-by-step that we could trust Him for everything that we need. I have asked Chester to write this part of our story.

PART 2
of
Twice Chosen

God Proves His Faithfulness

By Chester D. Kylstra

Introduction

I appreciate Betsy asking me to write a section for her book. After all, it is her book and she did not have to let me write any of it. But as you can probably see by now, she has a big heart, is gracious to everyone around her (including me) and gets in trouble every now and then because of her gift of mercy.

So my assignment is to share with you the story of God's faithfulness to us in the area of finances. Yes, that's right, I'm going to talk about money!

Some people, even good Christians, don't think that Christians should be interested in money.

"It's just not spiritual. It is crass, worldly, deceptive and the 'root of all evil.'[1] How could Betsy let such a subject be in her book?"

Well, we like to eat, have a roof over our heads, be warm, enjoy God's good earth and have money to give away. I suspect that you do also. In fact, Jesus makes it very clear in His parable about the unrighteous servant[2] that we are to handle "unrighteous mammon." It is **how** we handle the "mammon" that has a significant effect on our receiving "true riches" and that "which is our own,"[3] not how **much** we have.

One more thing. Betsy has already shared several significant parts of our financial testimony with you as she has told her story. However, since God has used this area of money in special ways to build our trust in Him, there are some additional important events and threads that we want to share.

So, let's launch into the story of God's teaching us His ways concerning money.

---

[1] The source of this common misconception is found in 1 Timothy 6:10.
[2] Luke 16:1-13
[3] Luke 16:11-12

Fixing a Fix

As Betsy has shared earlier,[1] in 1979 we left the safety and security of my employment at the University of Florida and her
employment at Santa Fe Community College in Gainesville,
Florida, for a fresh start in the mountains of North Carolina.
We left behind a significant and steady income for the uncer-
tain income of a consulting engineer and an air taxi pilot. We
also bought 110 beautiful acres of North Carolina mountainside, with a fabulous view of Celo Knob and the Black Mountain range across the Cane River valley.

We wanted a place where people could come to receive healing. Looking back on it now, it is clear that we were not even
close to being ready to provide a place of healing for others, we
were so wounded ourselves. But these were our immature, pre-
sumptuous steps of "faith," as we sought to follow God's leading and fulfill what was in our hearts.

Oh yes, we also went deeply into debt to buy this land.

Financially speaking, over the next two years, we sank slowly
out of sight. Actually, it happened rather rapidly.

First of all, we had counted on my many contacts in the university system, in the aerospace industry, and in government to
provide us with consulting contracts. Many of them had said
that if I ever had time for more consulting work, they would
really like to hire me. However, now that I had the time, they
seemed to not have the money. These contacts that were going
to provide me with large income consulting jobs disappeared.
That's right. They were gone. We were both shocked and
disappointed.

"Contracts, you remember those contracts that you wanted me
to sign? You know, the work that you so desperately needed to

---

[1] Please see page 80.

have done? That large consulting fee that you wanted to pay me? Don't you remember?!"

No, they did not remember.

Oh well, there was still the air taxi business!

"Mountain Air, at your service. Every seat a window seat. Clean, fresh, mountain air, gently blowing through the cabin. Quick, straight-line travel to wherever you want to go. You avoid all of those nasty, curvy, mountain roads. Mountain Air! We fly your schedule!"

Strange. People had an aversion to flying in the mountains, particularly at $40/hr. They would rather drive even if it did take them much longer!

However, there were some who did fly, but not enough of them. The air taxi business was slowly going broke. Actually, that happened rather rapidly also. The two "sure" things that we had counted on, the engineering consulting and the air taxi business, were not so sure after all!

Looking back on it now, we can see that God allowed us to get into a fix.

Have you ever had God "fix you a fix?" He is good at it. He doesn't even have to do anything. In fact, that is how He does it. He doesn't do anything. He draws back, lets us make our own choices and we end up in a fix.

In times like this we tend to turn our attention to Him. It seems that sometimes we humans just have to try to make it on our own, until we can't make it. Then, when we cry "Uncle," or better yet, "Help, God," He knows He has our undivided attention. He begins to work with us. He may even rescue us.

Dedication to God

As we breathed our last breath of financial air, we made a very important decision. We decided to give everything that we had and were to God. That included us, our family, our beautiful mountainside, our little cabins, our hopes and our dreams. And, oh yes, our consumer debts and our huge land debt.

In exchange, we received everything that God has and is. What a transaction!

This was a very serious thing to us. We were not playing games. We surrendered totally to God. We even wrote out an official agreement with God. Betsy and I both signed and dated it. It turned out to be a major, pivotal point in our lives, affecting us every way possible. Financially, it was our turning-around point.

A Little Bit Extra
Because of what we had already learned about God and His economy, we included in our agreement that we would give twelve and one half percent of our income to His kingdom. Why 12½% and not just the standard 10%, the "tithe," you might ask?

We felt that the tithe was essentially a minimum. It was our return to God, an expression of "Thank You" for the air we breathed, the sunshine we enjoyed, the food He provided, the family He put us in; in other words, all that He has done for us. It was a "Thank You" for all of the blessings that He had designed the universe to provide. We believed that our needs would be met as we tithed.

However, we wanted to give God the opportunity to bless us more than "just" having our needs met. We wanted to be blessed abundantly.[1] We were emotionally bruised from our years of "sinking out of sight," and we were ready for blessings.

---

[1] 2 Corinthians 9:8

We wanted to move into the arena of offerings, where we gave more than the ten percent. We had a lot of debt and we needed a lot of "blessings" to pay it off.

Yet it was hard to sow a lot of money to reap a harvest of even more money, when we didn't have any income to sow. So we pledged in our agreement with God that we would set aside 12½% of all that would come in. We even opened another checking account, our "Special" checking account, so that we would have it ready to immediately transfer 12½% of our income (if we should have any) into it.

Out of Debt!

Well, it was neat. Almost immediately, Betsy got a job at the local mental health center. Even though they did not want to hire a woman, she got the job. It was good for them, good for the people that she counseled and good for us. It was **income**.

Mine took a little longer. But a couple of months later I just "happened" to find out about a small aerospace company about 50 miles away. One day I walked into the Personnel Director's office with resume in hand. The next day I was the Chief Scientist's Assistant, with an **income**.

Over the next eight months, we paid off every consumer debt that we had accumulated. It was a sizable amount of money, but we were committed to honoring our agreement with God by paying it off as rapidly as possible. It was clear that He was doing His part. We kept our word as well to not fail Him.

Working as an Engineer
I drove fifty miles one way to work for four years. I was the resident software engineer at Stencil Aero Engineering, an ejection seat manufacturing company. (These ejection seats were used in navy fighter jets.) This company had used computers very little in their design and testing work. When they wanted to try out a new idea, they would actually build whatever was necessary and then launch the ejection seat out of a rocket sled to see how it worked. Very expensive!

They were eager to benefit from the savings that would occur by trying out new ideas on the computer before trying them with hardware. Only after the idea was provenned and refined by computer simulation would they need to spend the money for a "live" test.

I got to do all sorts of delightful things, such as creating six-degree-of-freedom trajectory simulation programs to model how the ejection seat with all of its various systems would function under different ejection situations. I had this job for the next four years, until the Lord called us to Bible College to prepare for the ministry.

An Experiment in
Fast Growing Seed

God was rapidly maturing us, showing us His ways in a number of areas, including finances. I was developing a series of teachings on God's Law of Sowing and Reaping as applied to prosperity when our pastor, Don Blankenship, asked me to teach a three-part series on finances. What an opportunity to share what God had been teaching us!

As Betsy and I prayed and asked the Lord what and how He would have us do the teaching, I felt like He was challenging us to give a one dollar bill to each person. I felt that we were to take a step of faith and give away our money so that others could have the experience of planting and then watching God rapidly bring in the harvest.

My first reaction to this challenge was, "Boy, I hope not too many people come to this class!" My next thought was, "I wonder if this really is God?" Then I got a grip on myself and asked God the really important question. "Is there a way to share this with Betsy so that she will agree that this is Your idea and not mine?"

We had three wonderful Sunday nights of teaching. At the end of the first session we explained to everyone that God wanted to demonstrate His law of Sowing and Reaping by challenging us to have faith for a rapid maturing of some "money" seed. People were visibly shocked when we explained that we were going to give a one dollar bill to each one. I could see that they were having the same thought that I had had. "Just how much money are we talking about here?!"

We had brought about $60 in brand new, fresh, right-out-of-the-wrapper, crisp, one dollar bills; as good as the Federal Reserve makes. We handed them out to the young, we handed them out to the old. Everybody got one. Then we prayed.

We asked God to speak to us, showing each one of us where He wanted us to plant our dollar bill. We asked Him to multiply it rapidly, so rapidly that we would already have testimonies about harvesting by the next Sunday meeting.

One neat thing God did as we listened for His voice was to speak clearly to Amy, the pastor's youngest daughter, age five. She had never heard God's voice before and that night God spoke to her clearly, telling her where to plant her seed. She was so excited, much more over hearing God's voice than having a dollar to plant!

Well, God was as good as His Word. We did have testimonies the next Sunday, and the following Sunday, and the Sunday after that, and even for a number of following Sundays. One woman kept replanting her harvests and after about 9 weeks, she had a new car! People had money coming in from all kinds of unexpected sources. It really was a supernatural happening as God demonstrated His faithfulness to fulfill His Rhema Word.[1]

A Word of Caution

It is time for a caution here, dear reader. The above experiment was a specific thing that God had us do. When God speaks to our heart with a specific Word, faith is ignited, our expectancy grows and He then manifests His goodness here on the earth. He spoke to us to give away the seed dollars and that He would multiply them—rapidly. We encourage you to be involved with God's economy by planting seeds of all kinds, but do it as the Holy Spirit directs you, with His Rhema Word to you, not with the Rhema Word that He gave to us (or to anyone else).

---

[1] God's Rhema Word is a specific word to a specific individual (or group) at a specific time. It usually "rings" as truth in the person's heart. It is not a general word, such as the Logos (written) Word.

Out of Debt! (Again)

It was fun and a relief being out of debt, at least as far as our consumer debts were concerned. But there was still that huge debt on our beautiful mountainside. Even though our bank accounts were growing now and the financial pressure had slacked off considerably, there was that very large once-a-year payment due on the land.

As the time approached each year, we would scratch around, a little here and a little there, but it was difficult to get enough "scratch" together to cover the bill. It was a time of great stress. We sought God.

"Why can't You bring forth some more rapidly-multiplying seed to take care of this crushing payment?"

We began to realize that we had gotten ahead of God. Like Moses, we had tried to start our ministry based on the desires of our hearts, before we were ready, rather than on God's leading. God needed to prepare us, first by healing us and setting us free of many bondages and mindsets and then by equipping us.[1]

At this time, God was allowing "life," based on our choices, to wean us from the land. The day came when we "explained" to God that we wanted "whatever He wanted," more than we wanted the land.

When the time was right, He brought a buyer and we sold the 110 acres at a respectable profit. Now we were totally out of debt, with a good amount of savings in the bank.

We had learned a number of valuable lessons, one of the biggest being that no physical object was worth the stress of "unpayable debt."

We had a very nice nest egg in the bank after selling the land. We rented a house that last year in the mountains, while God

---

[1] Betsy has shared about this process in Part 1, starting on page 103.

155

was convincing us that He really did want us in full-time ministry and that He had and would provided the funds to accomplish it. So finally, in the spring of 1984, we headed for Liberty
Bible College in Pensacola, Florida, with a new car, a station
wagon, a Ryder truck full of furniture, a job waiting for me and
a nice house we had rented on a scouting trip to Pensacola.

Sowing My Nest Egg

We took a much needed vacation before we actually arrived in Pensacola. One Sunday in Jackson, Wyoming, we attended a little Assembly of God church. During the worship service, the Holy Spirit spoke to me.

"Give that man in front of you your allowance."

Shock flooded me. I realized that I was about to lose my personal "piggy bank" again. I had accumulated my spending money for a number of months and had it in the form of a $100 bill in my billfold. "Oh no," I thought to myself, "Here we go again."

I really wanted to be obedient. After all, this was God speaking. Nothing but good would come out of this. But this was the second time now. It was like giving away part of myself, an expression of my freedom.

"Yes, Lord. I am happy to bless this man, whoever he may be."

A little later, the pastor had everyone greet each other. I shook the hand of the man in front of me and passed him a tightly folded $100 bill with the words,

"God told me to give this to you."

He was surprised, but accepted it without looking at it.

That night at the evening service, the man's wife thanked us profusely, explaining how her husband had been ready to "Give up on this Christian thing." He had about decided that God either didn't care or wasn't listening to him. The fact that I had given him $100 really floored him.

"Maybe God did care!"

When we got back to Pensacola, I reported for my new job. Guess what? The company had just declared bankruptcy and was closing its doors that week! No job!

While I did feel a fleeting, momentary tinge of regret for the company and its employees, my main thought was, "What about us, Lord?" Once again the spirit overrode the flesh. "God must have something better in store for us."

The 100 Fold Return

As we made our last trip to North Carolina to clean up loose ends before settling in at Bible College, I went by to see my former employer at the ejection seat company.

"We are so glad to see you. Where have you been? We have been looking all over for you," they said.

What a greeting! I felt like the found "lost coin."[1] It seemed that my absence had made their hearts grow fonder.

Well, not quite. It turned out that they had a rush job to do for the Navy on one of their ejection seat contracts involving a two-seat fighter trainer aircraft. There was concern about the possibility of the pilots colliding after they ejected, if there wasn't enough of a time delay between the ejection of the two seats. Yet, on the other hand, they wanted the timing delay as short as possible, so that the pilot ejecting last would still get out as quickly as possible, before it was too late.

A lot of variables affected the potential hazard that needed to be considered. The most important variable had to do with which pilot pulled the ejection handle first and thus went out first: the front pilot or the rear one. Also important was the weight of each pilot. Was he heavy, light, or in between? Other factors such as the speed of the jet and whether it was maneuvering or not, had to be included.

The six-degree-of-freedom ejection seat simulation program that I had developed for them was for an aircraft with one pilot, not two. They needed me to make the necessary modifications to the computer program, do the analysis and present the results in graphical form so the decision of the appropriate time delay could be made.

---

[1] Luke 15:8-9

They continued full speed ahead. "How soon can you start? We need the results in five weeks. Can you do it? We will pay you a good consulting fee!"

Hot Computers

Well, dear heart, while Betsy "sweated" in the front of the rented house in Pensacola with the broken air conditioners and four bored children,[1] I "sweated" in the back bedroom, laboring over my "hot" computers.

Every morning I would download over the phone line the results of the night's computations from the "big" computer in North Carolina. I would process and analyze the data, write and/or change the computer programs to further process the data, and then in the evening upload to North Carolina the programs and data for the next round of computations.

This was the summer of 1984. The IBM PC was just beginning to become popular and the IBM AT machine had just been introduced. Computer phone communications were "very" slow in those days and not at all reliable like they are today. There were lots of problems. I worked day and night for those five weeks, making Betsy a "consulting widow," but the job was accomplished and our bank account was "filled with plenty."[2]

I might add that the results made everybody happy. They showed that a nine-second delay between the ejection of the first and second seats would insure both pilot's safety under all conditions.

Along about the fifth week, as I was working in the back room wrapping up the project, the Holy Spirit spoke one day and said,

"How much is one hundred times one hundred?"

I said, "Ten thousand, of course."

"How much are you getting paid for this job?"

---

[1] Please see Betsy's description of this period starting on page 100.

[2] Proverbs 3:10

"Lord, you know that they are paying me ten thousand dollars."

"How much did I ask you to give away out there in Wyoming?"

"You had me give away my entire 'I don't-have-to-account-to-anybody' allowance. All one hundred dollars of it!"

"How much is one hundred times one hundred?"

"Lord, I just said ..."

Oh, one hundred times a hundred. Ten thousand. Ten thousand dollars! **The hundred fold return!**

"You had me give away that one hundred dollars because you knew that the company that had hired me was going to go bankrupt and that we would need another job and that the ejection seat company was going to need help and ... Oh, thank You, Lord. You are so good to us. You know the end from the beginning! Thank you for teaching us about the Law of Sowing and Reaping"

Double Your Giving

As the end of 1984 approached, we had completed our first semester at Bible College. We had another consulting job, providing a small, but steady, subsistence level of income. With another child entering college the next fall (for a total of three plus ourselves), we were calculating budgets, making plans, seeing what we could do to minimize our expenses and thus our needed income for the 1985 and 1986 school years.

I spent several days praying about our budget, asking the Lord if what we were coming up with was okay. Did we need to trim it a little more here or there? Were we overlooking something?

"What do you think, Lord? Are we on track?"

On the third day I heard a clear voice say, "Why are you being so stingy?"

I was surprised, even shocked! "Huh?"

"Why are you being so stingy?"

I felt confused. "What do You mean, Lord? Being stingy? We are just trying to be responsible, to be good stewards of Your money. We are trying to not be greedy and not spend money on things that aren't necessary."

"What about all the missionaries out there? What about the various ministries that depend on people like you? What about your church, that needs your help to accomplish the work that I have given it to do? How are they going to fulfill their purposes if you don't do your part, if you just think of yourself and your selfish 'minimum budget'?"

"Well Lord, we have included a tithe in our budget. But we didn't feel that we should ask for the extra, the offerings, for the next year or two."

162

I will never forget what the Lord said to me next. It penetrated into the depths of my being. It still resonates there today. He said,

"If you will double your giving, I will double your income!"

As the saying goes, "It doesn't take a rocket scientist to figure this one out." Actually, since I am a rocket scientist, it didn't take me very long either. I immediately saw that we had been approaching our budget from a position of "lack," rather than "abundance," and that God was displeased with our false, faithless, "sense of responsibility," and "pious stewardship."

"Yes Sir," I said. "We have a deal."

We immediately started "double" tithing, in spite of three children and two parents in school.

A Word of Caution (Again)
Again, dear reader, this was a specific Rhema word to us for a specific time. God may not be telling you to double your giving. It is more likely that He has something else for you to do. The key is to know what He wants each of us to do, and then to do it.[1]

---

[1] Isaiah 1:19

The Time of Testing

Do you know that when God's Word comes with a promise or a command, it always brings a time of testing. Our favorite examples of this are Joseph and David. Joseph became Prime Minister over all Egypt by way of the pit, accusation and prison.[1] David's preparation to become king over all of Israel included having the king throw spears at him and hunt him down like a fox. He also got to live in caves, act crazy before a Philistine king and have outlaws as his "subjects."[2] It makes one think twice about receiving a tremendous promise or "Word" from God, doesn't it.

The basic issue raised by a promise from God is, "Is God's Word true or not?" Everything and everybody will try (not necessarily intentionally) to make you give up on the promise or be disobedient to the command. This problem seems to go back to the Garden, where the serpent said, "Hath God said?"[3] We were double tithing, but, "Where was the 'double income'?"

The consulting job that I mentioned in the previous chapter continued through the following April. We were slowly depleting our savings from the sale of our mountain top. But after April, the slow tickle became a flood. I looked around for other consulting jobs, but to no avail. Betsy also couldn't find anything that would fit with being a college student. I made a couple of hundred dollars here and there, but it was not the amount that we needed.

By August, with five of us poised to start the college school year, our precious savings went under $1000. I estimated that we had about two to four weeks left and then, "back into debt!" We had developed a strong aversion to debt, particularly when we didn't know how we were going to pay it off!

"Lord, anytime you want to start the 'double income,' it's okay with us."

---

[1] Genesis 37, 39-41
[2] 1 Samuel 16, 18-31
[3] Genesis 3:1

164

The Gates are Opened

How many times have we heard it said, "God may not be early, but He is never late." This time He was right on time.

Here We Go Again

We were in church one Sunday, enjoying the worship, when the Holy Spirit said, "See that man over there?"

"Yeah, I see him." A sinking feeling started to develop in the pit of my stomach.

"Give him some money."

I pulled out my wallet and looked to see what I had. There was a twenty in the "family" side of it. It was clear that this was not what He had in mind. In my personal side, there was a $100 bill that I had again accumulated from my allowance money.

I was getting to be a "pro" by now, so I said, "Yes, Lord, I will be happy to give my-very-own-personal-money to that man. I'll do it right after the service."

I removed the $100 bill, folded it up and prayed a prayer of blessing over it.

The woman next to me (on the other side from Betsy), whom I did not know at the time, reached over and clasped both of her hands over my hands and let out a torrent of Holy Spirit prayer. I didn't know what she was saying, but I sensed it was good. In my spirit I then heard,

"Because you have been obedient to My voice, this day I am opening the Gates of Fort Walton Beach to you."

I knew immediately what God meant. In the Bible, the "gate of the city" was the place where the city fathers gathered to conduct the business of the city. It was the place of authority, power, prestige and money. God was opening a door that would lead to financial reward in Fort Walton Beach.

Eglin Air Force Base was located at Fort Walton Beach, with lots of advanced research and development going on. I had been over there the week earlier, going by and leaving my resume with over twenty aerospace contractors. God was guaranteeing that somebody over there needed me!

Sowing and Reaping

When I handed the designated man the $100 after the service, he profusely thanked me, expressing that he had not known how he was going to finish paying his college tuition for the fall. The $100 would complete his payment.

"Interesting," I thought to myself, "here we are needing college tuition for the five of us and God has me give away $100 to help pay someone else's tuition. It appears that God is having me put the Law of Sowing and Reaping to work again!"

The Phone Call

The following Tuesday, the phone rang.

"Hi there. This is Bud at Computer Science Corp. We were just awarded a contract and we want to get you started immediately. How soon can you come over? We need to get the paper work going to bring your security clearance up-to-date."

Friday morning, we negotiated a consulting contract. They wanted to hire me full-time, but I didn't want to drive 60 miles to work and back each day. Four years of long distance commuting in the mountains was enough. Besides, I had already agreed to teach "Science and the Bible" at the Bible College that fall and I needed a day for preparation and teaching.

We settled on my working four days a week at home on my computer and then coming over to Fort Walton Beach one day every week or so. For that four days of work, they agreed to pay me a rate that was almost exactly **double** the amount of income we had in the budget I had presented to the Lord the previous year. Actually, it was about 5% higher. I figured that the Lord had thrown in a little extra for seven months of inflation!

Continued Increase

Over the next three years, as we continued in Bible College and became involved in training counselors, God moved me through several jobs. I worked for Computer Science Corporation as a consultant, then as an employee and then as a consultant again. I also held a temporary, visiting professorship position at the University of West Florida in the Computer Science department for a couple of years.

Every time I changed jobs, the income would increase. We kept putting twenty percent (the "double tithe") into God's "Special" account. Ten percent, the tithe, went to our local church. For the rest, we wrote checks on it as the Holy Spirit would direct. We received a deep sense of satisfaction as we sent the money to various missionaries, ministries and churches.

For two years, we "peaked" out with all six of us in college. Then James, followed by Lewis, completed their degrees and the college expenses begin to decrease. There was always the money needed to cover the bills and keep food on the table. We were continually thankful to the Lord.

The Time of Testing (Again)

We received several prophecies about God's providing all of the finances we would need for the ministry He was giving to us. We knew that the prophetic word is accompanied by a time of testing, as I stated earlier, but we also had the promise of His doubling our income. I had accepted this promise fully by now. I wondered what He was going to do to keep our income increasing at the same time that we faced possible testing of our faith from the more recent Rhema Words.

It was during this time period that we had the crisis with Lewis' school bill of $4500, through which the Lord had us provide a way for Nina to attend Bible College. This was a major test of our faith, but one that did bless us and still does. Betsy has already shared this portion of our financial testimony with you.[1]

In the spring of 1988, the Holy Spirit said,

"Don't go back to the University of West Florida next fall. Let them know that your 'temporary visit' as a visiting professor is over."

We didn't know it at the time, but this was the end of secular work being a major factor in our lives. Our income began to decrease, not increase, for the first time in three years. For the last two years at Bible College, I had only a few small, short-duration, consulting jobs to nourish our bank account. Betsy continued teaching in the Bible College and working as Counselor to Women at the church, which brought in some money. The Holy Spirit began to have us accept contributions for the counseling we were doing, but most people did not contribute at all.

Looking back, I can not explain to you how we survived, but we always had enough. We skirted along the boundary between having a little surplus or having a little debt. On the average, we just broke even.

[1] Please see Betsy's account of this starting on page 114.

Ruined Testimony

Betsy was distressed. "Lord, what about our financial testimony? We are still double tithing, but where is the double income?" Silence, for what seemed like a long time.

Then one day, the Lord spoke to her.

> Are you more interested in preserving your 'financial testimony,' or in serving and knowing Me? Is your faith in your testimony, or in Me? Who is responsible for you, the 'financial testimony,' or Me?

"Forgive us, Lord. Forgive us for our complaining. Whatever it takes for You to conform us, to prepare us, that is what we want."

The Road into the Ministry

As Betsy has related in Part 1, we did survive the final Bible College years and begin to move more and more into active ministry. On the one hand we were in the ministry "full-time," but on the other hand we had periods with no income from ministry. We continued to believe God's promises for provision, that the time of testing would come to an end, and that there would eventually be finances to support the vision and activities that God was placing in our hearts.

The Gates are Opened (Again)

Betsy has told you about the Prophetic Counseling Conference sponsored by CI Ministries in March of 1994.[1] God used Bishop Bill Hamon and CI Ministries to thrust us into a more prominent public place, to give the Christian Prophetic Prayer Counseling ministry a broader exposure within the Body of Christ.

We believe that it also marked the end of the financial testing time. It is interesting that March, 1994, is about seven years from the time we began to receive prophetic words about abundance and prosperity, particularly for the ministry. Does "7", the number of completion, represent the completion of the testing time? Our earlier period of testing lasted seven months. Maybe we are moving into a higher level of finances, with a seven year rather than seven months testing time.

Since that conference, there has been a steady increase in the funds flowing through our hands, both for ourselves personally and for our ministry organization, "Proclaiming His Word, Inc." We are having both spiritual and material blessings as we are able to minister to more and more people, as God has opened the door for additional seminars throughout the United States. He has blessed the work of our hands as people have wanted to use the resources that we have developed for training counselors. He has surrounded us with able ministers,[2] both counselors and trainers, to multiply the impact of the ministry. We believe that God has again given us the "gate of the city" as He gave us the gates of Fort Walton Beach. Only this time, the gate is opening to the entire world.

As we continue to pray for and believe God's promises for ourselves and for those working with us, we expect that the finances needed to fulfill His Call, Commissioning and Vision will be available.

[1] Please see page 143 for Betsy's account of this event.
[2] 2 Corinthians 3:6

If there is anything that we have learned, it is that **God is Faithful.** All of His promises are **"Yes,"** and we join with Paul in shouting the agreement, **"Amen!"**[1]

---

[1] 2 Corinthians 1:20

PART 3
of
Twice Chosen

Into the Future

By Betsy Schenck Kylstra

God's Unfolding Plan

"What next?" people often ask us.

We have plans and we enjoy sharing them, yet we know so well that it is not, "How big?" or "How many?" or "Where?" that really matters. What matters is just what has always mattered: simple obedience to the Lord.

There are some things that the Lord has put on our hearts: such things as establishing regional training centers, providing scholarships to enable hurting Christian leaders to come to the Healing House for ministry and producing videos and additional resources to help train counseling teams. We expect there to be more reproduction of teams and much more networking.

In the winter of 1997, we will be piloting a new counseling model that has the potential of decreasing the amount of time spent in the counseling room without decreasing the level of personal healing. Eventually, we want to share this new model.

Ever since the missions conferences at Liberty Church, we have wanted to be involved in missions. In 1997, it looks like a portion of our time will be spent in other nations, primarily South Africa and Russia.

Both Chester and I have felt that there is something more that God wants to do in our lives and through our lives. Even though we are immensely fulfilled, there is an anticipation of something more. Last February (1996), Bishop Hamon prophesied over us, touching on this very issue.

> And the Lord says, Vision is coming. I've given you a world-wide vision, I've given you a world-wide burden, but I've only let you see through a glass darkly for the present. For the Lord says, Get ready, I'm going to start rolling up the shades and taking off the color and you'll see exactly what I want you to do. But I'm keeping the

blinds down until it's time; so just because you don't see how or when or where, that's because it's not time yet, says the Lord. When it's time, the window shades will go up and the sunlight will come in and the revelation will be there to go and do and be.

It is a very exciting time to be alive. God is pouring His Spirit out on the earth today. It is now over two years since His outpouring started in Lakeland, Florida, and in Toronto, Canada. People are still flooding to partake of it from all over the globe. Revival is occurring powerfully in many parts of our own nation. There were more than twelve-thousand salvation experiences during an eight-month period in Pensacola, Florida, at Brownsville Assembly. All denominations have been touched by it. There is revival in China and in South America, especially Argentina. Prayer teams are going to the 10-40 Window Nations[1] in preparation for revival there. It truly is the preparation for the end-time harvest.

We sense that the most satisfying years are still ahead. There are areas of ministry that both of us are drawn toward and some areas that we feel called to separately. Intercessory prayer is the area that I desire to grow in the most.

There is a translation of John 15:11 which best sums up all that I feel. Jesus is speaking to His disciples:

> These things have I spoken to you that the joy which is mine may be in you and that your joy may be filled full.[2]

"Thank You Lord for healing my dark side and through Your healing, bringing me into fullness of life. Thank You for all of those plans You had for me, which You said would be so fulfilling. They are. Thank you for letting me share in Your healing of other lives. Lord, thank You for **choosing** me."

---

[1] The 10-40 Window Nations are located at latitude 10° to 40° north, ranging from Africa to Asia. They are mostly unsaved, heavily populated nations.

[2] John 15:11, translation by Kenneth Wuest.

About the Author

(Bio updated for Third Printing, March, 2005)

God called Betsy and her husband Chester in mid-life from careers in aerospace software engineering and mental health counseling to new careers as teachers and counselors in the Body of Christ. During their preparation time at Liberty Bible College,[1] God both began to heal them and to reveal the elements of Christian Prophetic Prayer Counseling (CPPC). They started to counsel, teach and train other couples to function as counseling teams to help bring freedom and healing to church members.

Since 1990, when they began to minister full-time, God has continued to expand their vision. Besides counseling, they have established counseling programs within churches, conducted Healing/Deliverance, Activation, and Training Seminars throughout the USA and in other parts of the world, and trained counseling teams. In addition, they have been training others to minister as counselors and trainers within the local church.

They founded Proclaiming His Word, Inc., in 1992. God had said that others would be joining them and to prepare a covering organization to take care of them. This happened, with over sixteen trained counselors and trainers, as well as office staff, working with Proclaiming His Word by the end of the 1990s, as many leaders came to the CI/PHW Healing House in Santa Rosa Beach, FL.

In 2000, the Lord directed Chester and Betsy to release all those working with Proclaiming His Word into their own ministries and to launch the Healing House Network as the new covering ministry. This was done. There was also a name change, as

---

[1] Betsy has degrees in Counselor Education (MA, EdS). Chester has degrees in Mechanical (BS) and Nuclear Engineering (MS, PhD). They earned their Masters Degrees in Theology at Liberty Bible College, Pensacola, Florida.

177

Christian Prophetic Prayer Counseling became Restoring the Foundations (RTF) Ministry. By 2005, the number of qualified teams propagating the Restoring the Foundations ministry had grown to over 100. The Lord is using these teams to minister to leaders and others in the Body of Christ using the Restoring the Foundations ministry Integrated Approach, usually in an intensive, one-week ministry format. In addition, many church teams had been trained as Issue-Focused or Thorough Format ministers. They are serving their local churches, helping prepare the Bride without spot or wrinkle.

In 2004, the prophecies concerning an eventual training center came to fulfillment, as the Restoring the Foundations (RTF) International Training Center at Echo Mountain Inn in Hendersonville, NC, was birthed. It is allowing a great acceleration in the preparation and release of RTF ministers into the Body of Christ.

Betsy and Chester moved their ministry base from Santa Rosa Beach, Florida, to Hendersonville, North Carolina in 2004. They remain in association with Christian International Ministries and Bishop Bill Hamon, serving on the CI Board of Governers.

They have developed a number of resources to help train RTF ministers, with *Restoring the Foundations, Counseling by the Living Word*, the flagship training and self-ministry manual. Please visit their online store at www.phw.org for many of their resources as well as other resources designed to help train and to receive the Lord's healing and freedom.

Betsy and Chester have four adult children; James, Lewis, Eric and Pam.

You may contact Betsy and Chester through:

Proclaiming His Word Ministries
2849 Laurel Park Highway
Hendersonville, NC 28739

877-214-8076
office@phw.org
www.phw.org

You may learn more about the several ministries they have founded by going to the following web sites.

Proclaiming His Word Ministries

www.phw.org

Healing House Network   www.HealingHouse.org

RTF International Training Center

www.RTFTrainingCenter.org

Issue-Focused Ministry   www.IssueFocused.org

The RTF International Training Center is located at Echo Mountain Inn in Hendersonville, NC. This facility is operated year-round as a B&B inn. Please learn more at:

Echo Mountain Inn B&B   www.EchoInn.com

Printed in the United States
203609BV00003B/53/A